22

Audrey Hepburn

Portraits of an Icon

Audrey Hepburn

Portraits of an Icon

Terence Pepper and Helen Trompeteler

NATIONAL PORTRAIT GALLERY, LONDON

Contents

Acting Director's Foreword

I became aware of Audrey Hepburn at a very early age; I suppose you could say I was a fan, watching her films over and over – and then again later with my children – and being fascinated by her style, her sense of fun and her poise. I was privileged to be in the audience at the Barbican in 1991 when Audrey read from the diaries of Anne Frank, and where I was able to experience first-hand all of her mesmerising qualities.

It is not surprising that so many of the world's renowned photographers – Richard Avedon, Cecil Beaton, Philippe Halsman, Yousuf Karsh, Norman Parkinson and Irving Penn, to name but a few – have captured Audrey's inner radiance. In *Audrey Hepburn: Portraits of an Icon*, Terence Pepper, Senior Special Advisor on Photographs, and Helen Trompeteler, Associate Curator of Photographs, take us on Hepburn's journey from her early years in the Netherlands to her international stage and screen career, and finally her philanthropic work. Some of the photographs in this exhibition may be instantly recognisable, but others have rarely been seen before. Hepburn's strong sense of style, clearly evident in her association with the designer Hubert de Givenchy over more than forty years, and her creation of her own image can be seen throughout the exhibition and this catalogue.

The National Portrait Gallery also has an association with Hepburn. Sixty-five years ago, in 1950, Cecil Landeau's late-night production of *Petite Sauce Tartare* was performed in what was then the leading West End nightclub, Ciro's in Orange Street, now the home of the Gallery's Heinz Archive and Study Room.

It was a formative time for Hepburn, and set her on her journey to become an extremely successful international actress.

We are very grateful to Audrey's family and especially to her sons, Sean Hepburn Ferrer and Luca Dotti, who have collaborated with us throughout and have allowed us to display so many rare treasures. Thanks also to Michael O. Crain and Paul Alberghetti for all their help.

There are many colleagues at the Gallery who have worked towards this exhibition and I would like to express thanks to them all – particularly Rosie Wilson, Head of Exhibitions, and Eloise Stewart, Exhibitions Manager, who have managed the development of the exhibition, as well as Michael Barrett, Exhibitions Assistant, and Imogen Lyons, Research Assistant. Thanks also to all who have contributed to this catalogue: to Sarah Ruddick and Christopher Tinker for their editorial work, and to Ruth Müller-Wirth on the technical and production side. From the Communications team, thanks to Joanna Down, Claire Jackson, Nick Budden and Sylvia Ross, and to Jude Simmons for her elegant design for the exhibition. Other colleagues who have played a considerable part are Kathleen Bloomfield, Andrea Easey, Liz Smith, Fiona Smith, Sarah Tinsley, Helen Whiteoak; and Karl Lydon, Stuart Ager and their teams. I would also like to thank all our colleagues in Visitor Services.

I should like to offer particular thanks to all those private and public owners who have loaned important items, and to the *Audrey Hepburn*

Supporters Group who have helped make this exhibition possible. I would also like to thank the Bernard Lee Schwartz Foundation, whose generous gift in honour of Terence Pepper supported the preparation of this exhibition and catalogue, and in particular Michael Schwartz and Anne Varick Lauder for all their help.

I would especially like to thank Sandy Nairne, our Director until very recently, who gave great encouragement to colleagues to take this exhibition forward; and finally heartfelt thanks to Terence Pepper and Helen Trompeteler for giving us all such a wonderful opportunity to enjoy these images of Audrey Hepburn, who will continue to hold a very special place in the hearts of so many people throughout the world.

Pim Baxter
Acting Director
National Portrait Gallery, London

Curators' Preface and Acknowledgements

Terence Pepper

Photographs of Audrey Hepburn have long been a passion in my curatorial life at the National Portrait Gallery. The first portrait of Hepburn to enter the Collection was given by Cecil Beaton in 1968, while twenty-nine further portraits by him followed in 1991 from the estate of his secretary, Eileen Hose. Over thirty years ago, we acquired two prints by Norman Parkinson at the time of his first retrospective here, which I organised in 1981.

Hepburn has regularly featured in exhibitions at the Gallery, from *Stars of the British Screen* in 1986 to the book and television collaboration *The World's Most Photographed*, in which she was one of ten subjects explored. I was delighted when I first met Audrey Hepburn's son Luca Dotti after a lecture he gave in 2013 that he immediately recalled my featuring his mother on the cover of the definitive book accompanying my 2004 Beaton exhibition. Subsequent conversations with Sean Hepburn Ferrer and the custodians of the Audrey Hepburn Estate Collection have been equally inspiring and rewarding.

Audrey Hepburn inspired so many photographers to work creatively with her, and selecting works for this show with the Hepburn family and my very enthusiastic and hard-working co-curator Helen Trompeteler has been a journey of discovery, as more and more great images were discovered through persistent research and a great amount of support from all Gallery staff, generous lenders and others named elsewhere. I would particularly like to thank Imogen Lyons, who helped me prepare the original exhibition proposal and has since then assisted in organising and scanning several hundred pieces of historic ephemera including photographs, stills and rare magazines acquired through the internet and social media. I have also met a huge number of Audrey Hepburn fans active online, and four in particular have patiently supplied reams of fascinating research material: Gemma Cawley (audreyhepburnforever.tumblr.com) in London, Elizabeta Petukhova (timelessaudrey.tumblr.com) in Moscow, Meghan Friedlander (rareaudreyhepburn.com) in California, and Fernando Edouardo Sousa (thefashionofaudrey.tumblr.com) in Brazil.

Finally, thanks to Rosalind Crowe, who made frequent and helpful comments while we enjoyed watching almost thirty Hepburn films on DVD together.

Helen Trompeteler

As an award-winning actress and fashion icon, Audrey Hepburn continues to capture the public imagination. Her image has been immortalised on screen in over thirty films, and through enduring photographs by many of the most significant photographers of the twentieth century. Hepburn was pioneering in her use of her celebrity status to draw attention to humanitarian concerns; today, this great legacy continues through the work of her sons, Sean Hepburn Ferrer and Luca Dotti.

This exhibition follows in a tradition of major biographical shows at the National Portrait Gallery that examine the great lives of our time. The use of Hepburn's image was so prevalent and influential in her lifetime that for me, the opportunity presented by this exhibition was not only to consider Hepburn's life in photographs within a framework of photographic history, but also to contextualise the development of her image against a much wider social and cultural background. My desire to explore fully the interaction of such themes informed my curatorial approach and catalogue essay, which reflects on and celebrates Hepburn's remarkable cultural impact.

Audrey Hepburn: Portraits of an Icon has been made possible by the collective work of many individuals, too numerous to list here – however, I am grateful to them all. Firstly, thanks to my co-curator Terence Pepper for his collaboration on this project, and to Paul Moorhouse, Curator of Twentieth-Century Portraits, and Phillip Prodger, Head of Photographs, for our rewarding discussions. I am very grateful to Eloise Stewart, Sarah Ruddick, Michael Barrett, Imogen Lyons, Jude Simmons and Andrea Easey for their invaluable contributions. Further thanks also to my colleagues Clare Freestone, Georgia Atienza and Constantia Nicolaides. My work on this project is especially dedicated to Mr and Mrs M. Trompeteler, Paul Trompeteler, Dr and Mrs P. Ragg and family and Liz Dewar, who have been steadfast in their support and encouragement.

Acknowledgements

We are especially grateful to Audrey Hepburn's sons, Sean Hepburn Ferrer and Luca Dotti, for their support of this exhibition, and for generously loaning many exceptional prints. Our special thanks also to Robert Wolders, Audrey Hepburn's partner for the last decade of her life. At the Audrey Hepburn Estate Collection in California, we would like to thank Ellen Fontana, Nicole Slovinsky and Veronika Aiken, who contributed immeasurably to our research.

Many lending institutions, photographers' estates and private collectors have greatly contributed to this exhibition and publication. Our sincere thanks to Joanna Ling and Katherine Marshall at the Cecil Beaton Studio Archive at Sotheby's; Henry A. Blumenfeld and Nadia Charbit; Bob Adelman at the Howell Conant Archive; Matthew Cunningham and Robert Cooper; Shan Lancaster and Finn Hopson at the George Douglas Archive; Peter Fetterman; Philippe Garner; Sarah McDonald and Matthew Butson, Getty Images Archive; Malcolm Rogers, James Leighton, and Anne Havinga at the Museum of Fine Arts, Boston; William Klein and his studio manager, Pierre-Louis Denis; Steven Meisel and his studio; Alex Anthony and Elizabeth Smith at the Norman Parkinson Archive; Robin Morgan of Iconic Images and Terry O'Neill; Juliet Cuming and David Shaw at The Mark Shaw Photographic Archive; Melissa Stevens at the Sam Shaw Family Archives; Victor Skrebneski; and Christopher Willoughby.

We are also indebted to those individuals who have shared their knowledge and expertise, including Nigel Arthur at the British Film Institute; Russell Burrows and Bobbi Baker-Burrows; Simon Crocker; Brett Croft, Library and Archive Manager, Condé Nast Publications; Jerry Fielder and Julie Grahame; Inga Fraser; Jennifer Bello Roberts and the Halsman Family; Marissa Vassari at the New York Public Library; and Adrian Woodhouse and Richard Hill in connection with their work on Angus McBean's sitter books.

Introduction

I remember when my mother came to visit my first student flat in London. She was moved and I could not figure out why. Her dreamy eyes were seeing things that I could not see. The high street suddenly awoke images of her own formative years, a little-known time of her life.

For her, London had been a time for healing and hoping – a transition between childhood and adult life – tragedy and fame. She had left England with her mother at the onset of war. They came back with a hundred pounds in their pockets, after being on the verge of starvation during the Dutch 'Hunger Winter' of 1944–5.

Mother had been offered a scholarship at the Rambert Ballet School, but the dream of becoming a solo ballerina soon vanished. London however was no place for regrets. She got a gig in the chorus line of a show called *Sauce Tartare* at the Cambridge Theatre (the sequel was obviously *Sauce Piquante*), but it was not enough to make ends meet, not even living on the baked beans diet she enjoyed so much at the time. When the curtain came down she would therefore move with the other girls to Ciro's nightclub to perform in revues.

Like Eliza Doolittle, she had to learn it all. She had to learn how to speak, as the first line she ever pronounced on stage in *High Button Shoes* at the Hippodrome was barely audible. She had to learn to live with her flaws, real or imaginary: she thought she was too tall, her feet and ears too big and the rest of it definitely too flat. So when the great photographer

Antony Beauchamp bumped into her backstage at the Cambridge Theatre and asked if he could take a few pictures, she first declined politely, explaining that she could not afford them. The photos were published in British *Vogue*, and soon 'moonlighting' at Ciro's stopped being necessary.

It is therefore so fitting that that we can reconnect with that British girl so close to the former nightclub, which now hosts the public archives of the National Portrait Gallery. Passionate research has made it all possible: in fulfilling the Gallery's mission of retracing history through portraits, this thorough iconographic study, curated by Terence Pepper and Helen Trompeteler, allows me and my brother Sean to grasp fragments of an otherwise unreachable past.

The experience is all the more rewarding as the exhibition strives to go behind the scenes and provides rare insights into the making of a woman, following her rise from her London debut to the stardom of the fifties and sixties until the last season of her life, marked by restless humanitarian engagement on the frontline of forgotten crises.

She would be honoured to be here. And glad to be back home.

Luca Dotti

'No one can doubt that Audrey Hepburn's appearance succeeds because it embodies the spirit of today.'

Cecil Beaton

Audrey Hepburn: Becoming a Modern Icon

Helen Trompeteler

One of the most photographed actresses of her generation, Audrey Hepburn appeared in dance, theatre and television productions and over thirty films. Along with many other accolades, she received three Best Actress awards from the British Academy of Film and Television Arts (BAFTA) and was nominated five times for Academy Awards (Oscars), winning once for her performance in *Roman Holiday* (1953).[1] She possessed a determined work ethic and a distinct vision for her public identity, yet was always self-deprecating about her talents in published interviews. Recognised around the world as a fashion icon, Hepburn had a legendary style that appeared simple, achievable and sometimes even androgynous, yet it was unfailingly sophisticated. Such apparently chameleonic qualities enabled Hepburn to respond to and push against the gender expectations of her time, both through her film career and her carefully crafted image.

Many of the most significant photographers of the twentieth century, including Richard Avedon, Cecil Beaton, Angus McBean, Irving Penn and Norman Parkinson, attempted to capture Audrey Hepburn's elusive qualities. For some photographers, their portraits of Hepburn became defining images of their careers. Her multifaceted nature and her ability to redefine her image in response to changing cultural times made her a fascinating subject. For contemporary audiences, her persona remains intriguing because it resists easy characterisation.

Hepburn's iconic image as Holly Golightly in *Breakfast at Tiffany's* (1961) remains one of the most memorable representations of the 1960s (fig. 1). During this decade, artists such as Eduardo Paolozzi, Richard Hamilton, Jasper Johns and Robert Rauschenberg began to explore popular culture in the form of advertising, cinema, music, newspapers and magazines. They incorporated images of celebrities in their works, examining their resonance in the public consciousness.[2] Audrey Hepburn was one such star whose image permeated the cultural imagination, as exemplified by Dada artist Hannah Höch's photomontage *Homage to Riza Abasi* (1963; fig. 2). Höch responded to Hepburn's inherent adaptability by superimposing a newspaper clipping of Hepburn's face, originally printed in the German newspaper *B.Z.* on 10 November 1953 to coincide with the release of *Roman Holiday*, on to the image of a belly dancer.[3] By the mid-1960s, Hepburn's image had become so widely disseminated that artists such as Höch could treat her likeness as an emblem of womanhood and use it to explore universal themes.

How Hepburn reached this extraordinary level of cultural recognition can be understood through detailed examination of her photographic iconography, a relatively under-researched area compared to her contributions to film and fashion. Film was just one of the ways Hepburn's image was shaped, and arguably not the most enduring – during the most prolific period of Hepburn's career, in the days before films were routinely available through video or television broadcast, viewers might only experience a particular performance once. Photographic stills, however, were produced in the hundreds of thousands and widely featured in newspapers and picture-magazines in order to communicate a film's message and whichever qualities of a particular star the studios chose to feature. Such stills took several forms, including photographs made during the making of a film, later reconstructions intended to represent the look and feel of the production, and film-star publicity

portraits. Some of Hepburn's films, such as *Funny Face* (1957), mirrored her real-life experiences. These roles and their associated stills represent pivotal moments in the development of her image.

Discovery of a Chorus Girl: Britain 1948–51

From the 1920s onwards, improvements in the quality of film and photographic paper and the introduction of lighter, more sophisticated cameras resulted in new opportunities for photography to be distributed widely. During the Second World War, the effective use of photography in propaganda had demonstrated the power of the photographic image to influence ideas. This increased appreciation of photography coincided with advancements in printing technologies, and a new understanding of the importance of layout, typography and graphic design. Consequently, photography soon replaced text and illustration as the dominant medium for representing lifestyles in consumer magazines.[4] From the post-war years to the late 1950s, picture-magazines, including *Life* and *Look* in America, *Vu* and *Paris Match* in France, and *Illustrated* and *Picture Post* in Britain, became a vital source of information and entertainment. The popularity of such magazines coincided with the early days of television, and it was within this wider context that Hepburn began her professional career.

The nuanced expressions of movement that enchanted Hepburn's first audiences owed a considerable debt to her childhood ballet training in the Netherlands – at the Arnhem School of Music from 1941, and at Sonia Gaskell's studio on Zomerdijkstraat, Amsterdam, from the age of sixteen. In 1948, Hepburn's ambition to pursue a ballet career brought her to London, where she studied at Marie Rambert's prestigious school in Notting Hill. Hepburn later credited these ballet years for instilling her work ethic: 'Ballet is the most completely exhausting thing I have ever done, but if I hadn't been used to pushing myself that hard, I could never have managed the tremendous amount of work necessary to learn in three weeks how to play a leading role in my first real acting job.'[5]

On 22 December 1948, Hepburn made her London stage debut in the chorus line of the musical *High Button Shoes*. Theatrical impresario Cecil Landeau saw Hepburn perform and, recognising her potential, cast her in his revue *Sauce Tartare*. This ambitious production, which featured twenty-seven comic sketches and musical numbers, was a major success, enjoying 433 performances at the Cambridge Theatre, London. Hepburn returned in a larger role in its sequel *Sauce Piquante*, which led Ivor Brown of the *Observer* to write prophetically, 'the names of Joan Heal and Audrey Hepburn will someday be illuminated over theatre doors'.[6] *Sauce Tartare* and *Sauce Piquante* also brought Hepburn

to the attention of three photographers who would facilitate her wider discovery: society photographer Antony Beauchamp, renowned theatre photographer Angus McBean and photojournalist Bert Hardy. Hepburn's early photographs by these men provided the foundation of her public image as a figure whose natural beauty and personal qualities were to be admired. Hardy's photographs also signalled the major genre that would help define Hepburn's image throughout the 1950s: the picture-magazine photo-essay.

Antony Beauchamp (the son of miniaturist and photographer Vivienne) had begun his photographic career at the age of just sixteen, following the widespread reproduction of his photographs of Vivien Leigh at the time of her theatrical performance in *The Mask of Virtue* (1935). Further success followed with his regular series 'Crayon and Camera' for *Tatler*, and he later served as a war artist alongside fellow photographer Cecil Beaton. On seeing Hepburn perform in *Sauce Tartare* in 1949, Beauchamp was immediately captivated: '… all I was conscious of were the dancing eyes of that sprite in the chorus and for the rest of the evening I could scarcely take my eyes away from her face. I kept looking again and again at the startling eyes which were never still, which seemed to be brimming over with ebullient light-hearted joy.'[7]

Beauchamp had recently been commissioned to take photographs for an advertising campaign for department store Marshall & Snelgrove, and Hepburn's 'tall, slim, and curious, impish sort of attractiveness' struck him as suiting the assignment.[8] Beauchamp's resulting fashion studies, reproduced in the *Tatler and Bystander* (cats 6 and 7) and *Queen* between September and December 1949, did not name Hepburn, but they established her as one of London's most exciting new models. Beauchamp also photographed Hepburn in costume for *Sauce Tartare*, and on 14 September 1949 a portrait from this sitting was reproduced in the *Sketch* with Hepburn's name credited. Beauchamp later photographed Hepburn during the theatrical run of *Ondine* (1954) and the making of *War and Peace* (1956), and his personal tribute to her was published in *Illustrated* on 29 January 1955.[9]

Also in 1949, Angus McBean photographed Hepburn with cast members for *Sauce Tartare* and *Petite Sauce Tartare*. McBean had established himself as a highly inventive theatre and portrait photographer from the mid-1930s onwards, with his stage photographs regularly appearing in leading society magazines the *Sketch* and *Tatler*. A year after Hepburn's performances in *Sauce Tartare*, McBean was commissioned to create photographs as part of an advertising campaign for Crookes's Lacto-Calamine skin cream (fig. 3), and he remembered

the foundation

of summer beauty

Delicate skins can be a problem during the
summer months, especially at holiday time. The
cumulative effects of sun, sea or air tend to
remove the natural bloom of the skin, which
consequently becomes harsh and dry.
An application of Lacto-Calamine after sunbathing
brings immediate, soothing relief. Its soft,
cool milkiness penetrates deep down into the pores
and encourages ' skin-response ', a natural
reaction of the pores and cells to the stimulating,
healing influence from outside.
Lacto-Calamine is a medically prescribed
healing lotion, and can be used with the utmost
confidence in all cases of minor skin ailments.
It also makes the perfect powder base for
particularly sensitive skins.

CROOKES
Lacto-Calamine

 Inc. P. Tax. In the new easy-pour bottle. Replica handbag packs 1/9

54

2

3

Fig. 4
'We Take a Girl to Look
for Spring', *Picture Post*
(13 May 1950 issue),
photographed by Bert Hardy

Picture Post, 13 May, 1950

"Perhaps, If I Sit Quiet, It'll Come To Meet Me"

"Does It Ever Live For Long Inside A Tulip ?"

"Does It Need Another Frock ?"

Fig. 5
Picture Post cover
(15 December 1951 issue),
photographed by Bert Hardy

Hepburn's unusual gamine looks. The resulting photograph from October 1950 typifies McBean's signature surrealist style, which expertly used devices such as set design and props to great effect (cat. 13). McBean's use of a half-plate camera with 6 x 4 inch glass plates also enabled him to achieve compositions that were rich in tonal range and detail, ideal for reproduction on a large scale for theatre or advertising purposes.

McBean's idealised portrayal of Hepburn within an imaginary classical landscape was the first representation of the actress as a paragon of beauty. It was highly successful, appearing in British *Vogue* between May 1951 and August 1952 and in the *Tatler and Bystander* between June 1951 and August 1952, as well as in advertisements in pharmacies across the United Kingdom. A second alternative pose from this sitting showing Hepburn in a polka-dot swimming costume (fig. 40) was used in an additional campaign, published between March and July 1952.

McBean's photograph is an early landmark in Hepburn's iconography and remains one of his most popular images. As McBean acknowledged in his lifetime, the portrait has become forever linked with both their biographies: 'Perhaps if I ever go down in photographic history, it will be as the man who took the picture of Audrey Hepburn in the sand – so far it has appeared in every piece which has ever been written about me, and I am tied to it, like Steichen to the wonderful shot of Isadora Duncan in the Parthenon …'.[10]

In May 1950, Hepburn became the subject of her first photo-essay in a British picture-magazine when she was photographed by *Picture Post*'s Bert Hardy for the feature 'We Take a Girl to Look for Spring' (fig. 4). Established in 1938, two years after *Life* magazine, *Picture Post* enabled thousands of young people to learn about the culture and social concerns of their time. Hardy's photo-essay followed Hepburn on a tour of Kew Gardens and Richmond Park to regain the season she had missed due to her punishing schedule for *Sauce Piquante*. Taking a tour together with a young actress was an established promotion strategy: on 23 October 1948, *Picture Post* had promoted Ingrid Bergman with a similar story depicting Bergman being shown around London by her director, Alfred Hitchcock. Hardy's photographs emphasised Hepburn's modesty by often showing her tilting her head to avert the gaze of her onlooker, and the accompanying text stresses this girl-next-door appeal: 'she is very unself-conscious and friendly and sweet'.[11] These humble virtues were also highlighted by writers of the time, for example in *Illustrated* magazine, which described Hepburn as 'Twenty-two, brainy and beautiful, tantalizing and talented, she is a girl of

simple tastes …'.[12] Such idealism was occasionally tempered by acknowledgement of modern women's new aspirations and the pressures these created, as *Answers* magazine explained: 'Like all good artists she is always scared and worried about her work – worried that is, about whether it is good enough.'[13]

After the publication of such early magazine profiles, opportunities to appear in film soon followed, initially under the guidance of Robert Lennard, who had seen Hepburn perform in *Sauce Tartare*. As casting director for the Associated British Picture Corporation, Lennard was one of the most influential figures in British film. In an interview with *Picturegoer*, he recalled that 'sincerity and the willingness to work towards perfection' were the qualities he looked for in an actor. He found both in Hepburn: 'She was *working* all the time.… She was *alive* every second she was on the stage. And when she danced, her eyes danced, too.'[14] Lennard cast Hepburn for a small part in Mario Zampi's *Laughter in Paradise* and in *Young Wives' Tale* (both 1951). Minor roles followed in *The Lavender Hill Mob* (1951) and *Monte Carlo Baby* (1952), and Hepburn's film career was born.

Developing the Audrey Hepburn Look: America 1951–4

The formative years of Hepburn's career coincided with a time when the roles of women in society were continually being redefined. The Second World War had brought dramatic changes to perceptions of women; many had served in the armed forces or contributed to the war effort by doing jobs that were traditionally considered 'men's work', such as in civil-defence services, farming and industry. This new equality was transient, however, and during the early 1950s socio-cultural factors still exerted pressure on women to conform to traditional gender roles as wife and mother. This gender expectation is best illustrated by *Look* magazine's testament to the great American mother: 'The wondrous creature marries younger than ever, bears more babies and looks and acts far more feminine than the "emancipated" girl of the Twenties and Thirties. If she makes an old-fashioned choice and lovingly tends a garden and a bumper crop of children, she rates louder Hosannas than ever before.'[15] Against this cultural backdrop, Hepburn learnt to use fashion to define and control her image, and photography and its dissemination through international mass-circulation magazines came to promote her as a new alternative form of femininity.

Following her professional debut in Britain, in 1951 Hepburn found a mentor for the next stage of her career in acclaimed French writer Colette. While filming *Monte Carlo Baby*, Hepburn was staying at the Hôtel de Paris in Monaco. Colette, a fellow guest, was planning a stage version of her 1945 novella

Fig. 6
Posters for *Gigi* outside the Fulton Theatre, New York, 1951

Fig. 7
Hepburn with Paolo Carlini in *Roman Holiday* (released 1953)

Gigi with writer Anita Loos and producer Gilbert Miller, but the play was missing a lead actress. As Hepburn's biographer Barry Paris recounts, Colette observed Hepburn enjoying a break in filming in the hotel lobby, and she knew she had found her Gigi: 'What author ever expects to see one of his brain-children appear suddenly in the flesh … . This unknown young woman was my own thoroughly French Gigi come alive!'[16]

Hepburn's American stage debut in *Gigi* at the Fulton Theatre on Broadway (fig. 6) was marked by her first appearance in American *Vogue* at the age of twenty-two, with a portrait by Irving Penn published on 1 November 1951 (cat. 19). Penn had taken the portrait in Paris earlier that year, with further studies made with Colette at her Palais-Royal apartment. By this time, Penn had abandoned the motifs that had previously characterised his photographic style: formal, full-length compositions that relied on his 'corner structure' (created by joining two studio flats) or positioning subjects on a length of rough carpet. His new style, defined by tight cropping against a neutral backdrop, produced intense character studies. In the *Vogue* portrait, Penn's bold use of shape and Hepburn's natural simplicity combined to achieve a graphic effect especially suited to the magazine page.

Colette's endorsement of Hepburn established her credibility as a serious actress, and *Variety* quickly noted that she 'registers as a soon-to-be star, with looks, figure, acting skill, authority – and above all, personal magnetism'.[17] Colette extended her influence further by writing an exclusive feature, 'Hepburn … and Hepburn', for the *American Weekly*. Employing an elegant celestial theme, Colette compared Hepburn to a star in the ascendant, rising towards her great namesake Katharine Hepburn: 'When she finds her final place in the firmament, there will be two great stars named Hepburn, to the confusion of astronomers but to the delight of ordinary theatregoers.'[18] This analogy endowed Audrey Hepburn with the prestige of golden-era Hollywood at the very start of her career.

In June 1952, Hepburn began filming William Wyler's *Roman Holiday* on location, having successfully tested for the film the previous year. A Cinderella tale in reverse, *Roman Holiday* (1953) is the story of Ann (played by Hepburn), a disillusioned European princess who runs away for twenty-four hours to experience life. She falls in love with an American journalist, Joe Bradley (Gregory Peck), before returning to her royal duties. Hepburn's Oscar-winning role was the beginning of a long career with Paramount Pictures. The Cinderella motif established in *Roman Holiday* and reinforced by later films *Sabrina* and *Funny Face* would characterise Hepburn's public image for much of the 1950s. This

6

7

decade represented a new period of stability in the post-war years, and the infectious enthusiasm of Hepburn's performance in *Roman Holiday* as her character discovers the carefree pleasures of daily life reflected this new optimism. In a particularly symbolic scene Princess Ann has her shoulder-length hair cut into an elfin crop as an act of new-found freedom (fig. 7). It also coincides with the reality of Hepburn's own life, as the young actress began to develop her unconventional style.

As Hepburn was beginning her career in American cinema, Hollywood publicity portraiture was gradually introducing a new realism and moving away from the glamorous style characterised by master photographers such as George Hurrell and Clarence Sinclair Bull. Paramount had been the first of the major Hollywood studios to establish a permanent stills and portrait photography studio.[19] Photographer Bud Fraker had developed his career at Columbia Pictures in the early 1930s before joining Paramount in 1942 as an assistant to A.L. 'Whitey' Shafer. On Shafer's death in 1951, Fraker succeeded him as Director of Stills Photography. Like Penn's portrait at the time of *Gigi*, Fraker's head shots, costume and creative portraits of Hepburn were so successful because they captured the graphic elements of her face and silhouette with great attention to form, line and shape, ensuring arresting compositions that would withstand mass-production as publicity stills and in print (fig. 8). His work with Hepburn was notably documented by Bob Willoughby (cat. 25), who pioneered the use of photojournalism techniques in on-set film photography.

Within the restrictive environment of the Hollywood studio system, in which the major film studios cultivated and promoted their chosen actors and actresses under strict contracts, Hepburn maintained control of her evolving image by carefully managing her appearance. Legendary costume designer Edith Head, with whom Hepburn worked during the making of *Roman Holiday*, recalled to author Charles Higham: 'Like Dietrich, Audrey's fittings became the ten-hour not the ten-minute variety. She knew exactly how she wanted to look or what worked best for her, yet she was never arrogant or demanding.'[20]

Hepburn's next film, *Sabrina* (1954), was a modern-day Cinderella story of a chauffeur's daughter, Sabrina Fairchild (Hepburn), who for years had been in love with playboy David Larrabee (William Holden). After two years in Paris, Sabrina returns a sophisticated woman, eventually falling in love with David's older brother Linus (Humphrey Bogart). In the summer of 1953, Hepburn had visited Paris in preparation for this role and was introduced by Gladys de Segonzac (the wife of the head of Paramount's Paris office) to designer Hubert

de Givenchy. Hepburn chose three pieces from Givenchy's spring/summer collection for key scenes in the film to illustrate Sabrina's transformation. Edith Head also made costumes from a number of Givenchy's sketches. Paramount's contract with Head meant that Givenchy's designs were uncredited in the film, but in 1957 he was named in the credits for *Funny Face*. Hepburn's collaboration with Givenchy continued, with the designer producing pieces for her personal wardrobe and costumes for *Love in the Afternoon* (1957), *Breakfast at Tiffany's* (1961), *Charade* (1963), *Paris When It Sizzles* (1964) and *How to Steal a Million* (1966).

Hepburn became the embodiment of Givenchy's purity of style and understated sensuality (fig. 9). Their partnership transcended conventional roles of muse and designer, as Givenchy explained: 'She knew exactly what she wanted. She knew perfectly her visage and her body, their fine points and their faults … She wanted a bare-shouldered evening dress modified to hide the hollows behind her collarbone. What I invented for her eventually became a style so popular that I named it "*décolleté* Sabrina".'[21] This neckline was quickly imitated in store-bought versions that featured in US *Vogue*.[22]

After the release of *Sabrina*, *Picturegoer* magazine declared Hepburn 'the most individual actress since Garbo and the early Dietrich'[23] and *People* remarked that 'such a sparkling and accomplished young actress hasn't been found for the films for a long time'.[24] Givenchy's sophisticated elegance had established Hepburn as a unique star, far removed from the sexual 'pin-up' image of contemporaries such as Marilyn Monroe and Jane Russell. This shift was observed by *Silver Screen*: 'She's changing Hollywood's taste in girls. From the full-bosomed sweater-filling type with more curves than the New York Central Railroad, to the lean, umbrella-shaped variety … It may be that the accent has gone off sex slightly and gone on to femininity.'[25] The potency of Hepburn's new image was confirmed by critic Cynthia Lowry: 'It is no secret in the magazine world that a picture of the lady on a cover is like a Benzedrine pill to sales'.[26] *Vogue* summarised further: 'She has so captured the public imagination and the mood of the time that she has established a new standard of beauty, and every other face now approximates to the "Hepburn look" …'.[27]

The significance of *Sabrina* in the development of Hepburn's image is especially evident in the documentary cover story 'Audrey Hepburn: Many-sided Charmer' by Mark Shaw for *Life* magazine (7 December 1953). Shaw achieved an unprecedented level of access to Hepburn which allowed him to create the definitive record of the actress during the making of this film. The story originally started badly, with Hepburn avoiding Shaw's

Fig. 8
Photograph by Bud Fraker,
published in *Picturegoer*
(3 October 1953 issue)

Fig. 9
Photographed with
Hubert de Givenchy by
David Seymour, 1956

8

9

Fig. 10
Contact sheet of photographs
by Mark Shaw, taken during
the filming of *Sabrina*, 1953

cameras, but they soon reached an understanding: '…when she realized that photographer Shaw was trying to accomplish in his field what she was trying to do as an artist in hers, she forgot about *Life*'s cameras watching her closely day after day.'[28] Hepburn allowed him to publish the first pictures of her at home ever released for publication. Shaw worked closely with *Life*'s movie editor Mary Leatherbee to find a pattern of 'typical' Hepburn gestures, movements and expressions among his thousands of negatives, in order to capture the rare and elusive qualities of glamour and magnetism that excited Hepburn's audiences (fig. 10).

Shaw's work demonstrates the power of the photo-essay, by the mid-1950s, to shape public reputations. His photograph of Hepburn walking down a pathway in front of her Beverly Hills apartment (cat. 27) was repeatedly reproduced uncredited after its original publication. This alluring image invites engaging eye contact with the film star, yet Hepburn remains tantalisingly unatttainable as she turns away from the camera. In her choice of haircut and clothing Hepburn blurred boundaries between conventional depictions of male and female, and Shaw described the appeal of this style: 'Audrey is the most intriguingly childish, adult, feminine tomboy I've ever photographed … she's many women wrapped up in one …'.[29]

Hepburn transformed her image again with her Tony Award-winning role in *Ondine*, performed at the Forty-Sixth Street Theatre, New York, between February and June 1954. *Ondine* is the fable of a water-nymph (Hepburn) who falls in love with a knight (Mel Ferrer) only for him to betray her, resulting ultimately in his death and her return to her watery world. Portraits of Hepburn as *Ondine* include Philippe Halsman's provocative pose of Hepburn in a fishnet costume credited to designer Valentina Schlee (cat. 29).[30] A striking colour portrait by Antony Beauchamp reproduced on the cover of *Everybody's Weekly* (12 February 1955) showed Hepburn in costume for *Ondine* at The Cloisters Museum, New York (fig. 11). Hepburn was also photographed by Richard Avedon for *Harper's Bazaar* (cat. 30) with the accompanying image caption crediting 'the boon of her gazelle-eyed looks, her early-blooming theatrical *expertise*'.[31] Avedon's use of high contrast reduces Hepburn's face to its core elements, and the duality between dark and light cleverly echoes the duality of mortality and immortality experienced by Hepburn's stage character.

Hepburn's role in *Ondine* coincided with her developing relationship with actor Mel Ferrer, whom she later married in a civil ceremony in Buochs, Switzerland, on 24 September 1954; a religious ceremony recorded by Ernst Haas followed the next day in the small thirteenth-century church at nearby Bürgenstock. Haas's intimate photographs were published as the photo-essay 'Audrey writes the end to Cinderella' in *Picture Post* (16 October 1954). In December, Hepburn and Ferrer visited Britain and discussed making a film version of *Ondine* with celebrated directors Michael Powell and Emeric Pressburger. Noteworthy photographs of Hepburn from this time in England include those by Cecil Beaton published in the *Sketch* (26 January 1955), and studies with Ferrer in a Surrey winter landscape by Antony Beauchamp published in *Illustrated* magazine (29 January 1955). While the film version of *Ondine* remained unrealised, the staggering press coverage prompted by Hepburn's return visit to England demonstrated the British public's loyalty to the star they had first discovered.

International Stardom: 1954–9
By 1954 Hepburn had become an international film star and had fulfilled the promise of *Picturegoer*'s earlier prediction, 'The Future Belongs to Audrey'.[32] As the decade continued, Hepburn ambitiously sought to expand her repertoire as an actress. Writer Bernice Fitz-Gibbon described the dilemma perceived by many women at this time: 'Ambition is a tricky word. It's a word that started out being the same for both sexes and turned out to mean one thing for males and another for females. Ambition is an admirable thing in a young man.… But just try ambitious in front of the word woman. And what do you see? A grim single-minded dame with a ride-hard compulsion. You can be ambitious – but it must be a relaxed ambition …'. [33]

As her fame continued to grow, Hepburn was careful not to appear uncompromising in pursuing her ambitions. Mindful that mass-circulation magazines could help or harm her career, she took charge of her image, as *Illustrated* magazine reported: 'At the top of her career in her early twenties, and determined to stay there, Audrey has assured ideas about her appearance. She will not hesitate to advise a photographer about her best, and worst, camera angles, and which of his photographs he should publish, or destroy.'[34]

Acclaimed photographer Cecil Beaton celebrated Hepburn's unique appeal in a number of sittings throughout her career. His first sitting with the actress in 1954 produced some of his most enduring photographs, with poses including a study showing Hepburn bathed in dappled sunlight against a detailed fabric background (cat. 56). Also an accomplished writer and diarist, Beaton contributed to Hepburn's growing reputation with an article for British *Vogue* in which he praised her as a new feminine ideal: 'it took the rubble of Belgium, an English accent, and an American success to launch the striking personality that best exemplifies our new *Zeitgeist*.'[35]

Fig. 11
Photograph by Antony
Beauchamp published on the
cover of *Everybody's Weekly*
(12 February 1955 issue)

Fig. 12
Photograph by Mel Ferrer
of staff at Villa Rolli reading
an issue of *Paris Match*,
with a cover portrait by Willy
Rizzo, during the making of
War and Peace, 1955

11

12

Having established her career with a series of 'Cinderella' film roles, Hepburn was offered an opportunity to redefine her image in the part of Natasha opposite Mel Ferrer (Prince Andrei Bolkonsky) and Henry Fonda (Pierre Bezukhov) in *War and Peace* (1956). Filmed at Rome's famous Cinecittà studios at a cost of $6 million, the film retold Tolstoy's novel in an epic three-and-a-half-hour film. As the *Daily Sketch* enthused: 'This performance rescues Audrey Hepburn from the coils of whimsy which were threatening to hold her captive since *Roman Holiday.*'[36] The film's director, King Vidor, would later credit Laurette Taylor, Lillian Gish and Audrey Hepburn as the three actresses he believed most creative of all those he had directed throughout his career.[37]

With *War and Peace* came notable changes in the way Hepburn was photographed, echoing the growing impact of Italian neorealist cinema. Filmmakers including Vidor were abandoning the studio-bound confines of the Hollywood tradition to take their filmmaking onto the streets and emphasise everyday realities. Hepburn was increasingly photographed on location and at her rented farmhouse, the Villa Rolli at Cecchina, near Rome, by photographers including Norman Parkinson (cats 36 and 38), George Daniell (cat. 40) and Philippe Halsman. Halsman was frequently commissioned by international picture-magazines, and for *Life* alone he produced one hundred covers. His colour portrait of Hepburn, introducing a cover story for *Life* (18 July 1955), perfectly combines the glamour and intrigue necessary to invite a reader into the magazine (cat. 35), while his black-and-white study of Hepburn standing under an olive tree featured her quiet femininity (cat. 34). Here Hepburn raises her arms to mirror the shape of the branches immediately behind her and in the far distance, creating an appealing three-tiered composition anchoring her natural beauty within the Italian landscape.

Hepburn's pervasive influence is evident in George Daniell's atmospheric street photograph taken in Rome (cat. 39), showing a series of Lux soap advertisements incorporating an image of Hepburn by photographer Bud Fraker. Such was the cultural impact of Hepburn's image by the time *War and Peace* was released that newspapers carried advertisements from beauty salons promoting 'Natasha' cuts imitating the actress's style in the film. Stern's of New York declared their version 'a delightful flatterer that's exquisitely feminine, yet as easy-to-manage as it is lovely-to-look-at'[38] and Haggerty's salon ran similar advertisements for their adaptation in the *Los Angeles Times* in August 1956.

In February 1956 a fashion study of Hepburn by Erwin Blumenfeld originally created in 1952 was published in *Esquire* magazine (cat. 20). Shown

modelling a hat by milliner Mr Fred, Hepburn's head is repeated into an infinite distance using a series of mirrors. This composition addresses the frequently beguiling nature of Hepburn's image: 'Not knowing which is the real Audrey, the lens turned to a many-sided look: an interpretation phrased in the form of a question mark.'[39]

The film *Funny Face* (1957) saw Hepburn return to her dance training and the familiar Cinderella motif of earlier films. Both a celebration and satire of the fashion industry, the film blurred the distinctions between fiction and Hepburn's personal biography by exploring the roles of high fashion, photography and society magazines in shaping the development of a modern star.[40] *Funny Face* centred on fictitious photographer Dick Avery (Fred Astaire) and magazine editor Maggie Prescott (Kay Thompson), a character inspired by legendary real-life fashion editor of *Harper's Bazaar*, Diana Vreeland. Jo Stockton (Hepburn) is a shy bookshop clerk who is transformed into a couture model by Avery, who subsequently falls in love with her. The narrative was inspired by photographer Richard Avedon, who worked as visual consultant on the film. He produced a bold title sequence showing transparencies of fashion studies being laid over a lightbox, and provided colour stills for the film's photo-shoot sequences. Avedon also created the overexposed close-up of Hepburn's face that Avery recreates in the film's darkroom scene, which was later used in its poster designs.

To make *Funny Face*, director Stanley Donen used the widescreen VistaVision format and experimentally blended photography and film techniques. Pivotal moments in Jo's development are marked by photo shoots with Avery and key musical numbers, in which Donen intercut positive, negative and colourised freeze-frame stills and split-screen images into the scene. The culmination of Jo's physical and personal transformation is marked by a landmark scene in which she runs with arms outstretched down the steps of the Louvre in a red Givenchy gown, echoing the composition of the Winged Victory of Samothrace behind her (fig. 13). This dramatic juxtaposition renders Hepburn's image more powerful by its visual association with one of the most iconic artistic and mythological representations of female triumph.

Yousuf Karsh's photograph of Hepburn at Paramount Studios (cat. 42) presents an alternative to the many exuberant photographs of the actress taken during the making of this film. Hepburn is shown at a quiet, reflective moment when the demands of performance have subsided. Karsh recalled: 'I had expected to find her rather brittle, extremely sensitive, and always emotionally charged. So she is. Intensity, I suppose, is her particular quality and

Fig. 13
Photographed wearing a
red Givenchy gown in a
publicity photograph for
Funny Face (released 1957)

Fig. 14
Polaroid photograph taken by
Hepburn on location in Africa
during the making of *The
Nun's Story* (released 1959)

13

14

her particular success. Beauty is combined with an insatiable appetite for life, and for work too.'[41]

By the late 1950s, Hepburn was still finding herself cast in film roles typified by arrested adolescence or innocence, such as those of Ariane in Billy Wilder's *Love in the Afternoon* (1957) and Rima in Mel Ferrer's adaptation of W.H. Hudson's novel *Green Mansions* (1959). However, the role of Sister Luke in Fred Zinnemann's *The Nun's Story* (1959), based on Kathryn Hulme's best-selling novel, provided Hepburn with another opportunity to break free from this stereotype. Hepburn's character was inspired by the real-life story of Belgian nun Marie-Louise Habets, who worked as a nurse in the Belgian Congo before doubts about her faith led her to renounce her vows. Hepburn's performance was nominated for an Academy Award, and the *Daily Telegraph* described *The Nun's Story* as 'a film that restores one's faith in an art form, and by implication one's faith in human nature'.[42] The *New York Herald Tribune* credited the film as one of Hollywood's most mature achievements.[43]

Filming took place in Stanleyville in the Belgian Congo from January 1958. Hepburn's letters to Mel Ferrer and the many Polaroid photographs she took on location reveal what a transformative time the project was for her, both personally and professionally (fig. 14): 'Coming to Africa is certainly one of the greatest experiences in my life. Everything I see here and feel is so completely new and therefore constantly stimulating. Wherever the eye can see there is beauty in such a very visual way.'[44] Hepburn's research for the role had included observing operations at the Ospedale di San Giovanni in Rome, and four days of filming were spent at the leper colony run by the English missionary Dr Stanley Browne. The personal impact of arguably the most demanding role of Hepburn's career is suggested in Leo Fuchs's portrait of the actress, in which she conveys an unguarded vulnerability (cat. 47). Hepburn's strong connection with the role of Sister Luke would bring her back to Africa decades later in her role as a UNICEF ambassador.[45]

In 1959, shortly after Hepburn's return from filming, she and Avedon created one of their most distinctive collaborations, the portfolio 'Paris Pursuit' for *Harper's Bazaar*. (Cat. 55 is a photograph from this series, published in September 1959.) The portfolio took the form of an imaginary film, with a title page designed to look like film credits and fashion photographs staged to look like movie scenes complete with accompanying titles and dialogue. Exaggerated depictions of Hepburn as a schoolgirl with long, plaited pigtails reference the persistent adolescence of many of Hepburn's 1950s film roles. In one fictitious 'scene', Dallas (Mel Ferrer) sees

lookalikes of Jemima (Hepburn) across Paris, calling to mind the widespread imitation of the 'Hepburn look' (fig. 15). The happy ending of the portfolio's narrative sees Jemima re-find Dallas high up in the Italian Alps, mirroring perhaps the happiness Hepburn and Ferrer found privately at their home in Bürgenstock. Symbolically, 'Paris Pursuit' marked the laying to rest of an aspect of Hepburn's image that was repeatedly visited in the 1950s and acted as a bridge to the reinvention that would follow.

The Hepburn Look Reinvented: 1960–9
The 1960s was a revolutionary decade across many cultural fields including fashion, film, music and photography. The rise of popular satire and an emerging teenage youth culture challenged conventional thinking. Various socio-cultural events, such as D.H. Lawrence's novel *Lady Chatterley's Lover* (1928) finally being declared not obscene in November 1960, brought sexual politics to the forefront of public discussion in Britain. The aftermath of the adulterous affair of John Profumo, Secretary of State for War, with Christine Keeler was long-lasting, eventually contributing to the fall of Harold Macmillan's Conservative government in October 1963. Furthermore, the introduction of the contraceptive pill in America in 1960 and the United Kingdom in 1961 irrevocably changed women's lives. Such social changes prompted feminist writers, including Betty Friedan in *The Feminine Mystique* (1963), to explore new questions surrounding sexual liberation, personal happiness and societal expectations. While social change for many women at the start of the decade was slow, opportunities were gradually broadening, as noted by Helen Gurley Brown in her bestseller *Sex and the Single Girl* (1962): 'You may marry or you may not. In today's world that is no longer the big question for women.'[46] American cinema was already beginning to explore formerly taboo subjects with, for example, Elizabeth Taylor's portrayal of a model and call girl in *Butterfield 8* (1960). Hepburn knew she would have to take similar risks with her future career to compete in this changing cultural arena.

Meanwhile, in February 1960, she had accompanied Ferrer to Rome, where he was to star in the film *Blood and Roses*. Overlooking the city, Hepburn posed for Cecil Beaton wearing hats by the designer Tanessa of Rome (cat. 57). The resulting photographs were published in the *Daily Express* announcing 'The new grown-up face of Audrey Hepburn' with Beaton adding 'She has now a new womanly beauty.'[47] In July of the same year, Hepburn gave birth to a much-longed-for first child, Sean, and his official christening photographs were taken by long-time collaborator Richard Avedon.

The role that would enable Hepburn to dramatically reshape her public image was, as for Taylor, that of

Fig. 15
Audrey Hepburn as
Jemima Jones, with Mel
Ferrer in 'Paris Pursuit',
photographed by Richard
Avedon, August 1959

a call girl: Holly Golightly in Blake Edwards's *Breakfast at Tiffany's* (1961), adapted for the screen by George Axelrod from Truman Capote's novella. Capote had originally wanted Marilyn Monroe for the role, as her liberated public persona matched the character he had crafted. Despite Monroe's successful test scenes for Capote, however, her dramatic advisor Paula Strasberg counselled her against taking the part.[48] The film's producers, Martin Jurow and Richard Shepherd, offered it to Hepburn. The press observed 'Famed as a portrayer of princesses and nuns, Audrey is doing a 180-degree turn to play Holly Golightly, a wild, weird creation of Truman Capote',[49] and Hepburn was understandably cautious: 'I hesitated a long time before accepting the part … It's very difficult, and I didn't think I was right for it … It was Blake Edwards who finally persuaded me.'[50] At the same time, Hepburn was pragmatic about adapting to evolving tastes, as she explained to Earl Wilson in the *New York Post*: 'It's a cycle … you can only sell what the public's interested in. That's what it wants today …'.[51] Paramount publicist Cameron Shipp attempted to reduce Hepburn's risk in taking the part by issuing a press release emphasising Holly as just a 'kook', an independent spirit, and the film left many of the novella's sexual characterisations deliberately ambiguous.

The film's opening scene shows Hepburn gazing at Tiffany's window display on Fifth Avenue at dawn, wearing a dramatic black column gown by Givenchy (fig. 18). Hepburn's appearance and her poignant performance of Henry Mancini's 'Moon River' remain landmarks in modern cinema history. Ironically, the role of 'the kookiest hipster ever to make the grade as a Hollywood heroine' recast Hepburn as a worldly sophisticate.[52] Many women searching for independence and happiness amid the confusion of a new era identified with *Breakfast at Tiffany's*, and Hepburn's status as a modern icon was secured. The film was also fundamental in representing New York as a symbol of opportunity, as the novelist Joan Didion later summarised in her essay 'Farewell to the Enchanted City' (1967): 'It was an infinitely romantic notion, the mysterious nexus of all love and money and power, the shining and perishable dream itself.'[53] Howell Conant's photographs of Hepburn in his Manhattan studio (cat. 59) and on location at Tiffany's (cat. 58) provide a definitive document of this important role. Hepburn and Conant later collaborated on fashion studies including those for *Life* (20 April 1962) and *Ladies' Home Journal* (September 1963), and Conant also photographed her at the time of the thriller *Wait Until Dark* (1967, cat. 71).

Hepburn's new maturity as an actress was marked by other roles around this time, including her only Western, John Huston's *The Unforgiven* (1960), and her portrayal of a school teacher facing rumours of a lesbian relationship in William Wyler's *The Children's Hour* (1961). She momentarily revisited the theme of transformation for the popular film *My Fair Lady* (1964), which saw the return of photographer Cecil Beaton to produce Edwardian costume designs incorporating the graphic sensibilities of new 1960s Op art.

Hepburn's range expanded further with comedic roles in Stanley Donen's *Charade* (1963), Richard Quine's *Paris When It Sizzles* (1964) and Wyler's *How to Steal a Million* (1966). This last film, made from July 1965 at the Studios de Boulogne, Paris, saw Hepburn portray Nicole Bonnet, the daughter of an art forger, who enlists art thief Simon Dermott (Peter O'Toole) to recover a forged Cellini statue. Famed hairdresser Alexandre of Paris created a new haircut for the occasion, the 'Coupe Infante '66'.

Such was public interest in Hepburn's image that the cut's measurements were reported in American *Vogue* (¼ inch at the ears, ⁷⁄₈ inch on the sides, top 2¾ inches, bangs 4¾ inches, neck 2³⁄₈ inches) alongside portraits by William Klein.[54] Make-up artist Alberto de Rossi introduced the heavy use of eyeliner that completed Hepburn's dramatic Sixties look. The 'new Audrey Hepburn' received public approval on the film's release in July 1966, when a new opening-day record in the thirty-three-year history of Radio City Music Hall was set, with takings of $30,387 (equivalent to around £140,000 today). Douglas Kirkland's definitive Sixties portrait of Hepburn shows her in costume for the film's opening scene (cat. 65). Dressed in a white felt helmet, white Givenchy suit and holding oversized Oliver Goldsmith sunglasses, Hepburn is the epitome of mod fashion. Terry O'Neill also took photographs during the making of *How to Steal a Million*, including a portrait of Hepburn with Peter O'Toole (cat. 66).

The role of Joanna Wallace opposite Albert Finney as her on-screen husband in Stanley Donen's *Two for the Road* (1967) completed Hepburn's reinvention during the 1960s. The film's non-chronological narrative tells the story of an unsteady twelve-year marriage, which daringly includes her character's adultery. 'Audrey Hepburn Swings? You're Kidding' declared the *Ladies' Home Journal* in January 1967, in an article illustrated with photographs by Klein. For the film, Donen insisted Hepburn break with her trusted Givenchy, employing Ken Scott and later Lady Clare Rendlesham as fashion advisors. Twelve of the film's twenty-nine costumes were by Scott, including his signature print dresses. Costumes by a new generation of designers also included a black vinyl suit by Michèle Rosier for French fashion house V de V, Cacherel shirts, Mary Quant shifts, wrap-around glasses by André Courrèges and Paco Rabanne's now famous aluminium disc dress

Fig. 16
German publicity photograph for
Two for the Road (released 1967)

39

16

(fig. 16). Another new hairstyle was developed for Hepburn by Patricia Thomas, and Alberto de Rossi modified Hepburn's eye make-up. The contentious themes of the film (for the time) and Hepburn's engagement with new contemporary fashion designers confirmed her ongoing status as a cultural icon. Donen described Hepburn's metamorphosis: 'The Audrey of the last few weeks on this film I didn't even know. She overwhelmed me. She was so free, so happy. I never saw her like that. So young!'[55]

An Icon Endures

In 1968, Hepburn received what would be the final Oscar nomination of her career, for the thriller *Wait Until Dark*. In December of that year, her divorce from Mel Ferrer was finalised. She married Andrea Dotti, a young psychiatrist and assistant professor at the University of Rome, on 18 January 1969, and her second son, Luca, was born in February 1970. After enjoying an intensive film and stage career, Hepburn chose to withdraw from her public life as an actress to devote herself entirely to her family.

During Hepburn's retirement from full-time acting, she remained in the public eye in part due to the role of 'paparazzi' news photographers who documented her day-to-day life in Rome. Such photographers had recorded Hepburn on and off set during most of her career, and Pierluigi Praturlon became a particularly trusted favourite. In later years, paparazzi photographers helped maintain Hepburn's reputation as an arbiter of taste and fashion, capturing her at social events and while carrying out her daily activities wearing ready-to-wear fashions by designers including Givenchy, Yves Saint Laurent, Emilio Pucci and Valentino. Hepburn's home life at La Paisible in Switzerland is shown in a number of photographs by Henry Clarke originally published in British *Vogue* in June 1971. Hepburn appeared occasionally on screen in the following decades, including roles in *Robin and Marian* (1976), *Bloodline* (1979), Peter Bogdanovich's *They All Laughed* (1981) and finally in a cameo part for Steven Spielberg's *Always* (1989). Hepburn divorced Andrea Dotti in 1982, and her partner for the rest of her life was actor Robert Wolders.

Late studio fashion photographs of Hepburn include those made by Jacques Malignon for *Harper's Bazaar* (September 1981) and Gilles Bensimon for French *Elle* (March 1988). Hepburn's sitting with Steven Meisel for *Vanity Fair* in 1991 is especially poignant. A joyful photograph from this session shows Hepburn in a black shift dress with her arms raised in a dance-like pose (cat. 78), recalling childhood photographs of her performing ballet while living in wartime Arnhem (cats 2 and 3). The far background of Meisel's portrait shows details of a photographer's studio including lighting equipment and a screen, inviting viewers to reflect on a life lived in front of the camera. While Hepburn remained an inspiration to a new generation of photographers, her resolute focus in later years was her family and her role as a UNICEF ambassador. Hepburn's humanitarian work from March 1988 onwards took her to countries including Ethiopia, Turkey, Sudan, Bangladesh, Vietnam and Somalia, and she would come to describe this as her most important legacy. Her contribution to the arts and to humanitarian work was later recognised in 1992 when she was awarded the Presidential Medal of Freedom, the United States' highest civilian award.

The recurrent theme of personal and physical transformation in Hepburn's major film roles and the paradoxes she embodied continue to capture the public imagination today. Hepburn's ability to reinvent her image became emblematic for many women who were redefining their own identity within society during the 1950s and 1960s. The images from Hepburn's vast iconography that endure are those in which her vision and the photographer's combine to convey her distinctive mystique. As Richard Avedon eloquently reflected in August 1990: 'I am and forever will be devastated by the gift of Audrey Hepburn before my camera … I love her but I have always found her impossible to photograph … I cannot lift her to greater heights. She is already there. I can only record, I cannot interpret her. There is no going further than who she is … She has achieved in herself the ultimate portrait.'[56]

Fig. 17
Photographed with Richard
Avedon by Henry Wolf, 1959

Notes

1. Audrey Hepburn received BAFTA Best Actress awards for her performances in *Roman Holiday* (1953), *The Nun's Story* (1959) and *Charade* (1963). She was nominated for Oscars for Best Actress in a Leading Role for *Roman Holiday* (1953), *Sabrina* (1954), *The Nun's Story* (1959), *Breakfast at Tiffany's* (1961) and *Wait Until Dark* (1967), winning once, for her performance in *Roman Holiday*. In 1994 the Academy also awarded her the Jean Hersholt Humanitarian Award.

2. Paul Moorhouse, *Pop Art Portraits* (National Portrait Gallery, London, 2007).

3. Katharine Conley and Pierre Taminiaux, *Surrealism and Its Others*, Yale French Studies, Number 109 (Yale University Press, New Haven and London, 2006), p.12.

4. Thomas Michael Gunther, 'The Spread of Photography', *A New History of Photography*, ed. Michel Frizot (Konemann, Cologne, 1998), pp.554–80.

5. Henry Hewes, 'Broadway Postscript: Stars Who Danced', *Saturday Review of Literature*, 15 November 1952, p.28.

6. Ivor Brown, 'The Critic as a Pest?', *Observer*, 30 April 1950, p.6.

7. Antony Beauchamp, *Focus on Fame* (Odhams Press Ltd, London, 1958), pp.96–7.

8. Ibid., pp.97–8.

9. Antony Beauchamp, 'Audrey Hepburn's Charm', *Illustrated*, 29 January 1955, pp.22–4.

10. Frederic Woodbridge Wilson, *The Photographs of Angus McBean: From the Stage to the Surreal* (Thames & Hudson, London, 2009), p.144; Terence Pepper, *Angus McBean* (National Portrait Gallery, London, 2006), p.25.

11. 'We Take a Girl to Look for Spring', *Picture Post*, 13 May 1950, pp.43–5.

12. Charles Hamblett, 'Audrey – The Other Hepburn', *Illustrated*, 2 June 1951, p.24.

13. 'Meet Audrey Hepburn: Everything Happens To Her!', *Answers*, 8 December 1951.

14. 'The Man Who Found Hepburn', *Picturegoer*, 10 October 1952, p.33.

15. *Look* (1956) quoted in Peter Lewis, *The Fifties* (Heinemann, London, 1978), p.45.

16. Colette quoted in Barry Paris, *Audrey Hepburn* (Orion, London, 2003), p.60.

17. *Variety*, 26 November 1951.

18. Colette, 'Hepburn … and Hepburn', *American Weekly*, 23 March 1952, p.13.

19. Robert Dance and John Russell Taylor, *Glamour of the Gods: Photographs from the John Kobal Foundation* (Steidl, Göttingen, 2008; National Portrait Gallery, London, 2011), p.26.

20. Edith Head quoted in Paris, op. cit., p.107.

21. Hubert de Givenchy quoted in Pamela Clarke Keogh, *Audrey Style* (Harper Collins, New York, 1999), p.39.

22. 'Late-day choices – choicest when hatted', US *Vogue*, 15 November 1954, p.112.

23. 'Little Audrey makes me laugh and laugh', *Picturegoer*, 19 September 1954.

24. 'Great is the word for Audrey', *People*, 12 September 1954.

25. Earl Wilson, 'Is Hollywood shifting its accent on sex?', *Silver Screen*, July 1954, p.40.

26. Cynthia Lowry, 'Audrey Hepburn Seems to Be Sensation of Decade', *Louisville Courier Journal*, 21 March 1954, quoted in Paris, op. cit., p.107.

27. Nicholas Drake (ed.), *The Fifties in Vogue* (Henry Holt & Co., New York, 1987), quoted in Paris, op. cit., p.108.

28. Stanley Rayfield, 'The Girl Behind the Glamor' in *How Life gets the story* (Doubleday, New York, 1955), p.6.

29. Mark Shaw quoted in Vivian Brown, 'What's in Store in Glamour for '54', *Dodge City Daily Globe*, 23 December 1953, p.5.

30. Biographer Alexander Walker also asserts that the costume was devised by Hepburn and inspired by the illustrated tales of Hans Christian Andersen in *Audrey: Her Real Story* (Orion, London, 1995), p.128.

31. *Harper's Bazaar*, May 1954.

32. Front cover headline, *Picturegoer*, 11 October 1952.

33. Bernice Fitz-Gibbon, 'Getting there is all', *Glamour*, September 1956, p.164.

34. Dennis Holman, 'Mel and I …', *Illustrated*, 22 January 1955.

35. Cecil Beaton, 'Audrey Hepburn', British *Vogue*, October 1954, pp.150–1 (article continues on p.222).

36. Harold Conway, 'Moscow Burns While Hepburn Loves', *Daily Sketch*, November 1956.

37. 'King Vidor Recalls Making Hallelujah', *New York Herald Tribune*, international edition, 10 July 1962.

38. Advertisement by beauty salon Stern's of New York, *Sunday Times*, 19 August 1956.

39. *Esquire*, February 1956, p.35.

40. Damian Sutton, *Photography, Cinema, Memory: The Crystal Image of Time* (University of Minnesota Press, 2009), p.125.

41. Yousuf Karsh, *Portraits of Greatness* (Thomas Nelson & Sons, London, 1961), p.98.

42. Campbell Dixon, 'A Classic of the Screen', *Daily Telegraph*, 25 July 1959.

43. 'New Dimensions in Hollywood', *New York Herald Tribune*, 1959.

44. Audrey Hepburn to Mel Ferrer, private letter, 11 February 1958.

45. Luca Dotti and Ludovica Damiani (eds), *Audrey in Rome* (Harper Design, New York, 2013), p.12.

46. Helen Gurley Brown quoted in Sarah Gristwood, *Breakfast at Tiffany's: The Official 50th Anniversary Companion* (Rizzoli, New York, 2011), p.69.

47. Cecil Beaton, 'The new grown-up face of Audrey Hepburn', *Daily Express*, 12 February 1960.

48. Paris, op. cit., p.168.

49. Bob Thomas, 'Audrey Hepburn To Play Truman Capote Beatnikke', *Herald Statesman New York*, 26 September 1960.

50. Eugene Archer, 'Playgirl On the Town – "Breakfast at Tiffany's" Has Audrey Hepburn Moving About Manhattan', *New York Times*, 9 October 1960.

51. Earl Wilson, 'What the Public Wants …', *New York Post*, 5 October 1960.

52. Thomas Wiseman, 'Audrey Hepburn sets a new standard for wantons', *Sunday Express*, 22 October 1961.

53. Joan Didion, 'Farewell to the Enchanted City', *Saturday Evening Post*, 14 January 1967, p.65.

54. 'It's in Vogue – Screen's Fair Lady Loses Her Locks', *Long Island Press*, 14 August 1965; 'New Girl On The Beauty Scene: Audrey Hepburn With The Coupe Infante '66', *Vogue*, 15 August 1965.

55. 'Look at Audrey Hepburn Now!', *Ladies' Home Journal*, January 1967, p.111.

56. 'That girl with the eyes', *Interview*, August 1990, p.101.

Fig. 18
Hepburn as Holly Golightly in
Breakfast at Tiffany's (released
1961)

18

PLATES

Childhood
and Early
British Success
1929-52

1 AUDREY HEPBURN, 1938

2 DANCE RECITAL PHOTOGRAPH BY MANON VAN SUCHTELEN, 14 APRIL 1942   3 BALLET SCHOOL RECITAL IN ARNHEM, NETHERLANDS, 1944

4 AUDREY HEPBURN (FAR LEFT) AT A BALLET CLASS DURING THE SECOND WORLD WAR, PHOTOGRAPHED BY ARNOLD BOUVET, 1944

5 AUDREY HEPBURN SHORTLY AFTER THE LIBERATION OF THE NETHERLANDS, 1946

6 FASHION PHOTOGRAPH BY ANTONY BEAUCHAMP, 1949

7 FASHION PHOTOGRAPH BY ANTONY BEAUCHAMP, 1949

8 PHOTOGRAPHED BY BERT HARDY IN KEW GARDENS, LONDON, ON 30 APRIL 1950 FOR *PICTURE POST* (13 MAY 1950 ISSUE)

9 UNPUBLISHED PHOTOGRAPH BY BERT HARDY TAKEN IN RICHMOND PARK, LONDON, ON 30 APRIL 1950 FOR *PICTURE POST*

10 CAST PHOTOGRAPH FOR *SAUCE TARTARE* AT THE CAMBRIDGE THEATRE, LONDON, BY ANGUS MCBEAN, JUNE 1949
(LEFT TO RIGHT: AUDREY HEPBURN, CLAUDE HULBERT, AUD JOHANSEN, ENID SMEEDEN AND JOAN HEAL)

11 PROGRAMME COVER FOR CECIL LANDEAU'S *PETITE SAUCE TARTARE* AT CIRO'S CLUB, LONDON, PHOTOGRAPH BY ANGUS MCBEAN, 1949
(LEFT TO RIGHT: AUDREY HEPBURN, ENID SMEEDEN AND PATRICIA DARE)

12 ADVERTISING PHOTOGRAPH FOR LACTO-CALAMINE BY ANGUS MCBEAN, NOVEMBER 1950

13 ADVERTISING PHOTOGRAPH FOR LACTO-CALAMINE BY ANGUS MCBEAN, OCTOBER 1950

FIG. 19 AUDREY HEPBURN IN *LAUGHTER IN PARADISE*, COVER OF *ABC FILM REVIEW* (MARCH 1951 ISSUE)

American Stage and Film

1951-60

15 AUDREY HEPBURN AND COLETTE, PRESS PHOTOGRAPH FOR *FRANCE-SOIR*, PARIS, 1951

16 AUDREY HEPBURN PHOTOGRAPHED IN COSTUME AS GIGI AT THE FULTON THEATRE, NEW YORK, BY NORMAN PARKINSON, JANUARY 1952

17 AUDREY HEPBURN PHOTOGRAPHED IN HER DRESSING ROOM FOR *GIGI* AT THE FULTON THEATRE, NEW YORK, BY LARRY FRIED, 1951

Picture Post, 10 May, 1952

GIGI LOOKS AT NEW YORK

Photographed by GEORGE DOUGLAS

Last November, 22-year-old British star Audrey Hepburn went to Broadway to take the title rôle in a play called 'Gigi.' Her performance was rapturously acclaimed. Here, with her fiancé, she takes a look at the city she captivated from the stage.

She Flutters the Pigeons in Central Park
Audrey strolls with fiancé James Hanson, director of a British road transport company. (Below) Thirst-slaking at a drinking fountain—a job for two.

Another Hepburn Challenge
Behind, the Rockefeller Centre. In front, a bright future, including a contract with Paramount films.

FIG. 20 'GIGI LOOKS AT NEW YORK', PHOTO-ESSAY BY GEORGE DOUGLAS FOR *PICTURE POST*, MARCH 1952 (PUBLISHED IN 10 MAY 1952 ISSUE)

18 UNPUBLISHED PHOTOGRAPH OF AUDREY HEPBURN AT ROCKEFELLER CENTER, NEW YORK, BY GEORGE DOUGLAS, MARCH 1952

19 PHOTOGRAPHED BY IRVING PENN IN PARIS FOR AMERICAN *VOGUE* (1 NOVEMBER 1951 ISSUE)

20 PHOTOGRAPHED WEARING A HAT MADE BY MR FRED, DESIGNED AND PHOTOGRAPHED BY ERWIN BLUMENFELD, 1952

21 WILLIAM WYLER DIRECTING AUDREY HEPBURN AND GREGORY PECK ON THE SPANISH STEPS FOR *ROMAN HOLIDAY* (RELEASED 1953)

FIG. 21 COVER FOR *LE SOIR ILLUSTRÉ* (11 FEBRUARY 1954 ISSUE) SHOWING AUDREY HEPBURN AND GREGORY PECK IN *ROMAN HOLIDAY* IN FRONT OF THE BOCCA DELLA VERITÀ (MOUTH OF TRUTH)

22 AND 23 COSTUME TESTS FOR *SABRINA* (RELEASED 1954), 21 SEPTEMBER 1953

AUDREY HEPBURN

P4037-23

24 PUBLICITY PORTRAIT BY BUD FRAKER FOR *SABRINA*

25 BUD FRAKER PHOTOGRAPHING AUDREY HEPBURN IN THE PARAMOUNT STUDIO PORTRAIT GALLERY, HOLLYWOOD, PHOTOGRAPHED BY BOB WILLOUGHBY, 1953

26 PUBLICITY PORTRAIT BY BUD FRAKER FOR *SABRINA*

FIG. 22 PHOTOGRAPHED BY MARK SHAW DURING THE FILMING OF *SABRINA*, REPRODUCED ON THE COVER
OF THE SPANISH EDITION OF *LIFE* (26 APRIL 1954 ISSUE)

27 PHOTOGRAPHED BY MARK SHAW OUTSIDE HEPBURN'S BEVERLY HILLS APARTMENT DURING
THE FILMING OF *SABRINA*, FOR A PHOTO-ESSAY IN *LIFE* (7 DECEMBER 1953 ISSUE)

A l'ondine qui est devenue
Audrey.

affectueusement

Philippe Halsman.

29 PHOTOGRAPHED BY PHILIPPE HALSMAN AS ONDINE, 1954

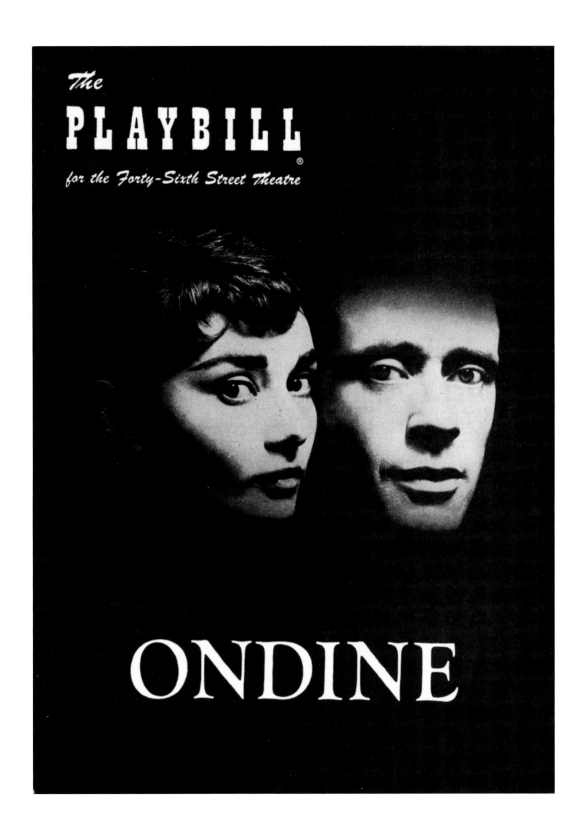

FIG. 23 PHOTOGRAPHED WITH MEL FERRER FOR THE PROGRAMME COVER FOR *ONDINE* AT THE FORTY-SIXTH STREET THEATRE, NEW YORK, 1954

30 AUDREY HEPBURN PHOTOGRAPHED BY RICHARD AVEDON, NEW YORK, 18 DECEMBER 1953

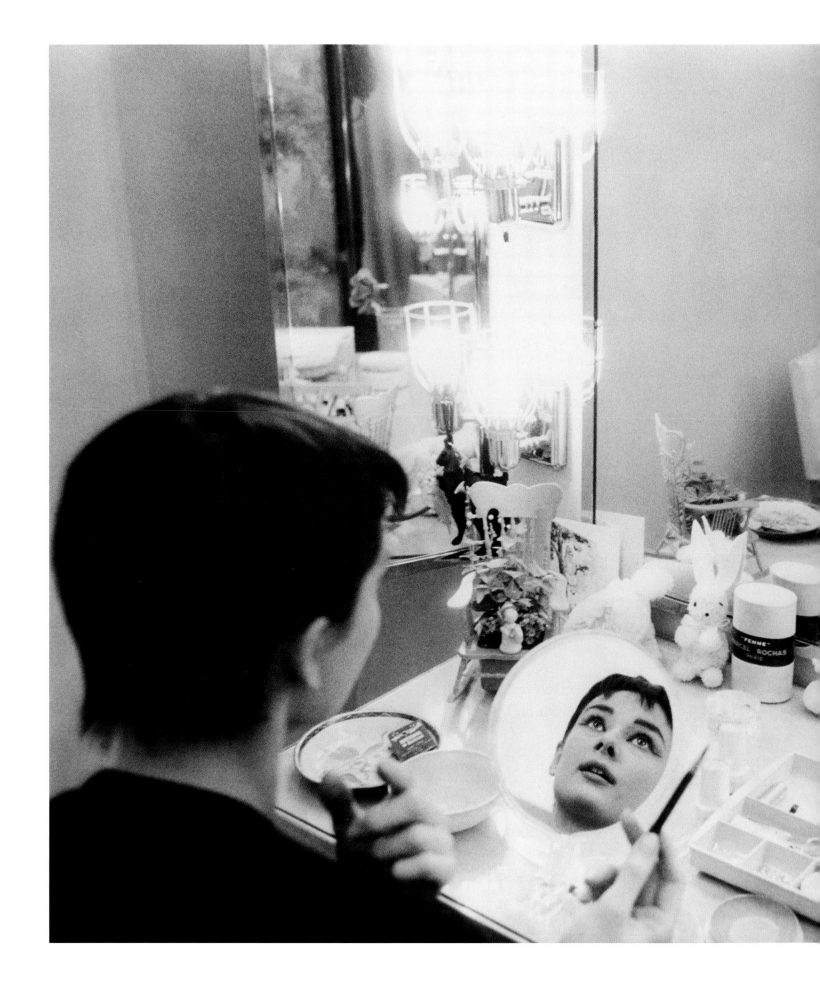

31 AUDREY HEPBURN PHOTOGRAPHED BY MARK SHAW PREPARING FOR *ONDINE* IN HER DRESSING ROOM
AT THE FORTY-SIXTH STREET THEATRE, NEW YORK, PUBLISHED IN *MADEMOISELLE* (JUNE 1954 ISSUE)

32 PHOTOGRAPHED BY ANTONY BEAUCHAMP, 1955

33 PHOTOGRAPHED BY ANTONY BEAUCHAMP, 1955

34 PHOTOGRAPHED BY PHILIPPE HALSMAN NEAR ROME FOR *LIFE* (18 JULY 1955 ISSUE)

35 PHOTOGRAPHED BY PHILIPPE HALSMAN NEAR ROME FOR *LIFE* (COVER PORTRAIT, 18 JULY 1955 ISSUE)

36 PHOTOGRAPHED BY NORMAN PARKINSON WITH BIMBA THE DONKEY AT THE VILLA ROLLI, CECCHINA, NEAR ROME,
DURING THE FILMING OF *WAR AND PEACE* (RELEASED 1956), 23 JUNE 1955

38 PHOTOGRAPHED BY NORMAN PARKINSON, WEARING GIVENCHY AT THE VILLA ROLLI, CECCHINA, NEAR ROME, DURING THE FILMING OF *WAR AND PEACE*, JUNE 1955

39 STREET SCENE IN ITALY PHOTOGRAPHED BY GEORGE DANIELL, 1955, SHOWING AUDREY HEPBURN IN POSTERS FOR LUX SOAP
(ADVERTISING PHOTOGRAPHS BY BUD FRAKER)

FIG. 24 HEPBURN WITH FRED ASTAIRE IN A PUBLICITY PHOTOGRAPH FOR *FUNNY FACE* (RELEASED 1957)

42 PHOTOGRAPHED BY YOUSUF KARSH, PARAMOUNT STUDIOS, HOLLYWOOD, 26 MARCH 1956

43 PHOTOGRAPHED BY SAM SHAW DURING THE FILMING OF *LOVE IN THE AFTERNOON*, 1956

44 PHOTOGRAPHED BY SAM SHAW DURING THE FILMING OF *LOVE IN THE AFTERNOON*, 1956

45 PHOTOGRAPHED BY GEORGE KONIG ON LOCATION IN THE GROUNDS OF THE CHATEAU VITRY, NEAR PARIS,
FOR *LOVE IN THE AFTERNOON* (RELEASED 1957)

PHOTO
RAYMOND
VOINQUEL

46 PHOTOGRAPHED BY RAYMOND VOINQUEL FOR *LOVE IN THE AFTERNOON*

47 PHOTOGRAPHED BY LEO FUCHS ON LOCATION IN AFRICA FOR *THE NUN'S STORY*, 1958

48 PHOTOGRAPHED BY HAMILTON MILLARD ON LOCATION IN AFRICA FOR *THE NUN'S STORY*, 1958

49　MEL FERRER DIRECTING AUDREY HEPBURN ON THE SET OF *GREEN MANSIONS* AT MGM STUDIOS, HOLLYWOOD,
PHOTOGRAPHED BY BOB WILLOUGHBY, 1958

50 AUDREY HEPBURN WITH HER FAWN, IP, IN GELSON'S SUPERMARKET, BEVERLY HILLS,
AT THE TIME OF FILMING *GREEN MANSIONS*, PHOTOGRAPHED BY BOB WILLOUGHBY, 1958

FIG. 25 AUDREY HEPBURN AND BURT LANCASTER ON LOCATION IN MEXICO FILMING *THE UNFORGIVEN* (RELEASED 1960)

51 PHOTOGRAPHED BY PHIL STERN ON LOCATION IN MEXICO FILMING *THE UNFORGIVEN* (RELEASED 1960)

52 DRAWING OF AUDREY HEPBURN BY CECIL BEATON, 1954

53 AUDREY HEPBURN AND RICHARD AVEDON PHOTOGRAPHED BY GERARD DECAUX, 1956

54 PHOTOGRAPH BY RICHARD AVEDON SHOWING AUDREY HEPBURN WITH A DRAWING OF HER BY RUFINO TAMAYO (MADE IN 1957)

55 AUDREY HEPBURN AND ART BUCHWALD WITH SIMONE D'AILLENCOURT, FREDERICK EBERSTADT, BARBARA MULLEN AND DR REGINALD KERNAN
EVENING DRESSES BY BALMAIN, DIOR AND PATOU. PHOTOGRAPH BY RICHARD AVEDON, MAXIM'S, PARIS, AUGUST 1959

57 PHOTOGRAPHED BY CECIL BEATON AT THE HASSLER HOTEL, ROME, JANUARY 1960

Film and
Fashion
Portraits
1960s

58 AUDREY HEPBURN AS HOLLY GOLIGHTLY AT TIFFANY'S FIFTH AVENUE, NEW YORK,
DURING THE FILMING OF *BREAKFAST AT TIFFANY'S* (RELEASED 1961), PHOTOGRAPHED BY HOWELL CONANT

59 AUDREY HEPBURN AS HOLLY GOLIGHTLY, PHOTOGRAPHED BY HOWELL CONANT IN HIS NEW YORK STUDIO, 1960

60 AUDREY HEPBURN AS HOLLY GOLIGHTLY ON SET DURING THE FILMING OF
BREAKFAST AT TIFFANY'S, PHOTOGRAPHED BY HOWELL CONANT

Shipboard switch to the twist by Audrey Hepburn

Audrey had a coiffured fringe on her face instead of her skirt, where orthodox twisters should have it, but there was nothing wrong with her technique. It delighted her husband, Mel Ferrer, at a charity ball aboard the new liner *France* in Le Havre. The ship didn't move but it didn't have to. Everything else did. Miss Hepburn had learned the twist in Paris. Aboard ship, her film, *Breakfast at Tiffany's*, was given its European premiere, but Audrey added a fillip to her screen performance with this one in the ballroom.

FIG. 26 AUDREY HEPBURN DANCING THE TWIST AT A CHARITY BALL ABOARD THE LINER *FRANCE* IN LE HAVRE, AT THE EUROPEAN PREMIERE OF *BREAKFAST AT TIFFANY'S*, PUBLISHED IN *LIFE* (26 JANUARY 1962 ISSUE)

61 AUDREY HEPBURN AND MEL FERRER, PHOTOGRAPHED BY PIERLUIGI PRATURLON, 1961

FIG. 27 AUDREY HEPBURN AND CARY GRANT IN A PUBLICITY PHOTOGRAPH FOR *CHARADE* (RELEASED 1963)

PHOTOGRAPHED BY VINCENT ROSSELL, WEARING A GIVENCHY SKI SUIT FOR *CHARADE*

63 AUDREY HEPBURN WEARING AN EMSEMBLE DESIGNED BY CECIL BEATON FOR *MY FAIR LADY* (RELEASED 1964), PHOTOGRAPHED BY BEATON, 1963

64 AUDREY HEPBURN ON THE SET OF *MY FAIR LADY* WITH HER DOG, ASSAM, PHOTOGRAPHED BY CECIL BEATON, 1963

65 AUDREY HEPBURN DRESSED IN GIVENCHY WITH SUNGLASSES BY OLIVER GOLDSMITH,
PHOTOGRAPHED BY DOUGLAS KIRKLAND FOR *HOW TO STEAL A MILLION* (RELEASED 1966)

66 AUDREY HEPBURN WITH PETER O'TOOLE, PHOTOGRAPHED BY TERRY O'NEILL DURING THE FILMING OF *HOW TO STEAL A MILLION*

FIG. 28 PHOTOGRAPHED WITH MEL FERRER BY BERT STERN FOR FRENCH *VOGUE* (MAY 1963 ISSUE)

67 AUDREY HEPBURN WEARING AN ENSEMBLE BY MICHELE ROSIER FOR V DE V AND BOOTS BY CELINE, PHOTOGRAPHED BY WILLIAM KLEIN FOR AMERICAN *VOGUE* (JANUARY 1966 ISSUE)

68 PUBLICITY PORTRAIT WITH ALBERT FINNEY FOR *TWO FOR THE ROAD* (RELEASED 1967)

CH-31(R83-5)

70 PUBLICITY PORTRAIT WITH SHIRLEY MACLAINE AND JAMES GARNER FOR *THE CHILDREN'S HOUR* (RELEASED 1961)

71 PHOTOGRAPHED BY HOWELL CONANT AT THE TIME OF *WAIT UNTIL DARK* (RELEASED 1967)

Legacy and
Later Years

1971-93

72 PHOTOGRAPHED WEARING GIVENCHY BY HENRY CLARKE FOR BRITISH *VOGUE* (1 MARCH 1971 ISSUE)

73 PHOTOGRAPHED AT HOME IN ROME BY ELISABETTA CATALANO, 1975

74 PHOTOGRAPHED WITH HUBERT DE GIVENCHY AT THE HOTEL LANCASTER, PARIS, BY VICTOR SKREBNESKI, 18 NOVEMBER 1986

75 PHOTOGRAPHED ON LOCATION IN PARIS WITH BEN GAZZARA FOR SIDNEY SHELDON'S *BLOODLINE* (RELEASED 1979)

76 PUBLICITY PHOTOGRAPH BY JOHN SHANNON FOR STEVEN SPIELBERG'S *ALWAYS* (RELEASED 1989)

PHOTOGRAPHED BY STEVEN MEISEL FOR *VANITY FAIR* (MAY 1991 ISSUE)

79 PHOTOGRAPHED BY ROBERT WOLDERS DURING A UNICEF MISSION TO SUDAN, 1989

'Success is like reaching an important birthday. You find you're exactly the same. All I feel is responsibility to live up to success, and, with luck, to survive it. The more I learn the better actress I shall be.'

Audrey Hepburn

Chronology

Terence Pepper

1929
4 May: Audrey Kathleen Ruston born at 48 rue Keyenveld, Ixelles, a small suburb of Brussels, Belgium, to a Dutch mother, Baroness Ella van Heemstra, and Anglo-Irish father, Joseph Victor Anthony Henry Ruston, one-time honorary British consul in the Dutch East Indies. She has two half-brothers, Ian and Alexander, from her mother's first marriage.

1935
May: Hepburn's father leaves the family, moving to London. She later recalls this as 'the most traumatic event in my life'. Terms of separation and custody dictate that Hepburn attend boarding school in England. Her mother has connections with the small town of Elham, near Folkestone in Kent, and in term-time 'little Audrey' lives in rooms at Orchard Cottage, Duck Street, owned by the local coal merchant and his wife, Mr and Mrs Butcher (who act *in loco parentis* when her mother is not visiting). She is enrolled in a small private school run by the six unmarried Rigden sisters and subsequently at a school in West Bank, near Elham Manor. One of the Rigdens is a disciple of Isadora Duncan and helps instil a love of dance in the young pupil.

1939
September: Outbreak of the Second World War. Hepburn's father changes his surname to Hepburn-Ruston, which relates to the Hepburn in his grandmother's family, tracing a connection to James Hepburn,

3rd Earl of Bothwell and third husband of Mary, Queen of Scots.

1940
29 January: After her parents' final divorce, Hepburn is relocated to the imagined comparative safety of Arnhem, in the Netherlands. The Baroness is involved in the arts council and appears with her family in an amateur theatrical event, in a Mozart tableau with eighteenth-century costumes and stage decor (fig. 31).

May: Invasion of the Netherlands by Germany. During five years of Nazi occupation Hepburn gives fund-raising dance performances for the Dutch Resistance. Her Uncle Otto is shot by the Nazis as a reprisal for resistance activity; her brother Alexander goes into hiding while Ian is sent to work in a munitions factory in Berlin.

1941
Previously interested in ballet from her school in England, Hepburn begins training under Winja Marova at the Arnhem Conservatory and becomes, with her mother's support, Marova's star pupil until the summer of 1944.

1944
17–26 September: Battle of Arnhem a disaster for the Allies. Destruction of the family's country home and the Arnhem Conservatory. The family is affected by the 'Hunger Winter', when very little food is available.

1945
4 May: Hepburn's sixteenth birthday coincides with the liberation of the Netherlands by Canadian troops. She moves with her mother to Amsterdam and joins the dance school run by Sonia Gaskell, then the Netherlands' most respected dance teacher, whose school later becomes the Dutch National Ballet.

1948
Early 1948: Two film-makers, director Charles Van der Linden and associate Henry M. Josephson, visit Hepburn at her dance classes, looking for a suitable actress to portray a KLM stewardess with an ability to speak in Dutch and English. Hepburn receives 50 guilders for her first film role. Titled *Nederlands in Zeven Lessen* (Dutch in Seven Lessons), the featurette mixes footage of Hepburn with aerial photography of the Dutch countryside to promote tourism.

7 May: The film premieres in the Netherlands. The Dutch version runs at 79 minutes, while the British version, *Dutch at the Double*, is abbreviated to 38 minutes. The film leads to modelling work at Tommy Waagemans' fashion salon in Amsterdam, and sittings with the artist Max Nauta.

8–22 May: The first magazine cover featuring Hepburn is published (fig. 32).

Late 1948: Hepburn travels to London to take up her scholarship at the Rambert

29

30

31

32

33

MARSHALL &
SNELGROVE
LONDON
The First Name in
Fashion

34

35

Fig. 33
Hepburn in the corps de ballet for *High Button Shoes*, photographed by Houston Rogers and featured in *Theatre World* (detail from March 1949 issue)

Fig. 34
Fashion advertisement for Marshall & Snelgrove department store, photographed by Antony Beauchamp and featured in *Queen* (9 November 1949 issue)

Fig. 35
Hepburn in *Sauce Tartare*, photographed by Antony Beauchamp and featured in the *Sketch* (14 September 1949 issue)

Fig. 36
Hepburn (far right) in *Christmas Party*, a revue at the Cambridge Theatre, London, with Gillian Moran and Cherry Adele in the Toy Shop scene, by Keystone Press, 9 December 1949

36

Ballet School in Notting Hill (previously the Mercury Theatre) and first lives at Marie Rambert's house in Campden Hill Gardens.

December: A career as a prima ballerina is ruled out by her above-average height (5 ft 7 in), and Hepburn leaves the Rambert School to apply for work in revues, musicals and fashion modelling in London.

She is chosen from over 1000 applicants to be one of ten chorus girls in the British production of the hit Broadway musical *High Button Shoes*, with choreography by Jerome Robbins and a score by Jule Styne. Other future stars in the production include Kay Kendall and Alma Cogan. After a preview run at the New Theatre in Oxford, the show premieres in London on 22 December and continues for 291 performances. Hepburn's one line was, 'Have they all gone?'

1949

March: A series of photographs of the production of *High Button Shoes* taken by Houston Rogers, which shows Hepburn in the corps de ballet, appears in *Theatre World*.

May: While in *High Button Shoes*, Hepburn is spotted by Cecil Landeau and recruited to be in his revue *Sauce Tartare*. The international cast includes Muriel Smith, the black star of *Carmen Jones*. The revue runs for 433 performances at the Cambridge Theatre.

September–December: Visitors to the show include the leading society and stage photographer Antony Beauchamp, who asks Hepburn to be one of six models for a major fashion advertising campaign for the Marshall & Snelgrove department store. After their first shoot Beauchamp decides to use only Hepburn for the campaign. The advertisements are published in *Queen*, *Tatler*, the *Sketch* and *Vogue* from 20 December 1949 until 20 January 1950.

20 December: During the Christmas period and until 20 January 1950 the *Sauce Tartare* cast perform matinees of a Christmas show, featuring Annette Mills and Muffin the Mule, while continuing with evening performances of *Sauce Tartare*. Hepburn plays the parts of the Christmas Doll and a Cossack.

1950

27 April: Hepburn is cast in Landeau's next revue, *Sauce Piquante*, at the Cambridge Theatre. The show runs for sixty-seven performances, closing in June. Hepburn's roles are enlarged and her salary increased. One of her roles is to carry a title card for each skit while dressed in a French maid's skimpy costume. During the run she is courted by the French-born star of the show, Marcel Le Bon, with a delivery of red roses on her 21st birthday and a rumoured engagement. Landeau intervenes, pointing to a 'no-marriage' clause in his dancers' contracts.

On Landeau's recommendation Hepburn has acting lessons with Felix Aylmer to expand her range of skills.

May: 'We Take a Girl to Look for Spring' in *Picture Post*, photographed by Bert Hardy, shows Hepburn in her first magazine photo-feature (fig. 4). An image from the shoot appears on the cover of *Picture Post* in December 1951 (fig. 5).

July: In a bid to offset the financial failure of *Sauce Piquante*, Landeau produces a shorter late-night version, *Petite Sauce Tartare*, at London's leading West End nightclub, Ciro's in Orange Street (now the home of the National Portrait Gallery Archive). The show is fronted by Muriel Smith but the programme cover features a photograph by Angus McBean of Hepburn and two other chorus girls. This was one of five occasions that Hepburn sat for McBean in relation to her early stage roles.

News of Hepburn's appearance in the revue at Ciro's quickly spreads around the British film community and subsequently several leading figures claim to have talent-spotted her. Among the most significant attendees are casting director Robert Lennard and director Mario Zampi, who sees Hepburn perform fourteen times.

Zampi offers Hepburn a major role in *Laughter in Paradise*, but she declines at first as she is rehearsing for a proposed touring show with Marcel Le Bon. When

37

this is cancelled, Le Bon leaves for America and Hepburn returns to Zampi to accept the part. The lead has been cast, but she is offered a smaller role as a cigarette girl, which she accepts. A colour photograph of Hepburn in costume appears on the cover of *ABC Film Review* in March 1951.

Autumn: *The Lavender Hill Mob* goes into production. In the opening sequence, set in a South American airport lounge, Hepburn approaches Alec Guinness to offer him a pack of cigarettes. Guinness is very impressed and introduces her to Hollywood director Mervyn LeRoy, then casting for *Quo Vadis*. Hepburn does a screen test for LeRoy, but the part goes instead to Deborah Kerr.

22 October: Hepburn has sittings with Angus McBean at his studio in Endell Street for a Crookes's Lacto-Calamine sun-lotion advertisement. The shoot utilises McBean's specially created surrealist set with miniature classical columns (cat. 13).

Late 1950: In the British film *Young Wives' Tale*, Hepburn plays a single woman living in a crowded house with two couples. At the film's wrap party she meets her future fiancé, James Hanson, a wealthy 28-year-old businessman from Yorkshire, who has previously dated Jean Simmons.

13 December: Hepburn's first appearance on a British magazine cover, with other actors contracted to Elstree Studios, in a Christmas-themed photograph taken by James Jarché for *Picturegoer*. The feature inside the magazine shows the group playing various Christmas games with Hepburn in a scene titled 'No Sad Songs for Me'. Jarché would later photograph her for *Picture Post* during the making of *Funny Face* in Paris.

1951
26 February: British director Thorold Dickinson offers Hepburn the part of Nora, a young ballet dancer, in the film *The Secret People*. He had seen her during the run of *Sauce Piquante* and auditioned her, but the offer is not made until four months into filming. It is her first big part in a major British film.

May: After completing post-production work on *The Secret People*, Hepburn travels to Monaco to film *Monte Carlo Baby* and its French version, *Nous irons à Monte Carlo*. While there she is seen by the legendary French writer Colette who is seeking an unknown actress to play the title role in *Gigi*, which has been adapted for the stage from her novella by Anita Loos. Colette insists Hepburn be offered the part.

First publication of advertisement for Crookes's Lacto-Calamine sun-lotion in British *Vogue*, featuring an uncredited Hepburn photographed by Angus McBean in October 1950. The campaign continues with a second photograph of Hepburn in a polka-dot swimsuit taken in November 1950 and published in summer 1952 (fig. 40).

2 June: Major feature in *Illustrated* magazine, written by Charles Hamblett and titled 'Audrey – The Other Hepburn'. The feature is illustrated with photographs by Joseph McKeown showing Hepburn on a day trip to Rottingdean in Sussex. Hamblett notes that Hepburn continues to travel to Ealing Studios by Underground from Marble Arch.

4 June: *Laughter in Paradise* released. It becomes the top-grossing British film of the year. Hepburn's line, 'Who wants a ciggie?', launches her British film career.

18 September: On the recommendation of Paramount's London production chief, Richard Mealand, Hepburn is asked to do a screen test for a major new film, *Roman Holiday*. The test is sent to William Wyler in Rome and Hepburn is offered the lead part and a contract for $12,500.

29 September: Hepburn sets off to New York on the *Queen Mary* on a five-day crossing to start rehearsals for *Gigi* (the passenger list includes her fiancé, James Hanson).

3 October: Hepburn is met at Pier 90 only by Morton Gottlieb, general manager for the play. She later comments that 'the first thing I saw when I came to America was the Statue of Liberty. The second [was the photographer] Richard Avedon …'. She is taken straight to Avedon's studio and then to modest accommodation at the Blackstone Hotel on East 58th Street.

· S P O T L I G H T ·

Piquante !

Sometimes one word is enough, and this time the word is "piquante." But in the revue "Sauce Piquante" at the Cambridge Theatre you'll find that in these costumes the girls symbolize other ideas. On the left, Audrey Hepburn as "Champagne" (read about her in Sidney Charteris's article) and right Patricia Dare as "Coq Noir."

Photographed by
PERCY KESSELL

11

38

Week ending December 23, 1950   EVERY THURSDAY THREEPENCE

Picturegoer
THE NATIONAL FILM WEEKLY

Picturegoer Christmas Party   see inside

39

40

41

42

43

44

Fig. 42
Photographed by Larry Fried
having coffee in New York
during rehearsals for *Gigi*,
late 1951

Fig. 43
Photographed by Larry Fried
in an automat in New York
during rehearsals for *Gigi*,
late 1951

Fig. 44
Winning *Theatre World*
Award for 'Most Promising
Personality' for her role in
Gigi (group includes Tony
Bavaar, Helen Wood and
Julie Harris)

1 November: To coincide with the play's opening, Irving Penn's portrait of Hepburn, photographed earlier in Paris, is published in American *Vogue*. The first preview performance of *Gigi* is given at the Walnut Theatre in Philadelphia on 8 November and it opens at the Fulton Theatre on Broadway on 24 November. A review by Brooks Atkinson of the *New York Times* describes Hepburn as 'a young actress of charm, honesty and talent', and Walter Kerr in the *New York Herald Tribune* writes that she brings 'candid innocence and tomboy intelligence to a part that might have gone sticky, and her performance comes like a breath of air in a stifling season'.

December: During the run of *Gigi* Hepburn continues dance instruction at the Tarassova School of Ballet on West 54th Street, run by Mme Olga Tarassova (whom she had known in Amsterdam three years earlier) and her husband Vladimir Bell. During a dance session Hepburn is photographed by Ben Ross for *Parade*. She is also photographed for a photo-essay by Larry Fried, who shows her alone in New York, at a coffee bar and an automat. George Douglas travels from London to photograph Hepburn in Central Park, at Rockefeller Center and backstage for a feature in *Picture Post*.

1952

13 April: Broadcast of TV Workshop Series 'Rainy Day in Paradise Junction', in which Hepburn plays Virginia Forsight, a crippled 16-year-old with dreams of a dancing career in Hollywood.

20 May: Hepburn wins the *Theatre World* Award for 'Most Promising Personality' for her role in *Gigi*, and is photographed with other winners.

31 May: *Gigi* closes on Broadway after 217 performances. Paramount give the play's producer, Gilbert Miller, $50,000 to release Hepburn from her contract in order to start filming *Roman Holiday* in Italy. During the run of the play Hepburn has meetings with Edith Head to discuss costumes for *Roman Holiday* and begins a long-term friendship. Straight from closing night in New York, Hepburn boards RMS *Queen Elizabeth* to meet director William Wyler, co-star Gregory Peck and the rest of the crew in Rome.

June: While filming, Hepburn lives in a flat in via Bon Compagni with her mother and James Hanson. Early scenes include filming at the Spanish Steps, where crowds of 40,000 onlookers have to be held back.

Images from Larry Fried's 1951 photo-essay are published in *Esquire* magazine.

30 September: Having completed work on *Roman Holiday*, Hepburn travels to New York, via England, to begin her tour of *Gigi*. Her planned wedding to Hanson is postponed due to her busy schedule.
13 October: *Gigi* opens at the Nixon Theatre in Pittsburgh and tours for eight months, visiting Boston, Cleveland, Chicago, Detroit, Washington and Los Angeles.

19 October: Hepburn's engagement to James Hanson is officially broken off, although she still spends Christmas in Chicago with him.

1953

16 May: The *Gigi* tour ends in San Francisco.

23 July: Hepburn attends a party held at her mother's apartment at 65 South Audley Street, Mayfair (where Hepburn also lives when in London). Other guests include Cecil Beaton, who writes in his diary that he has been 'wowed' by her; and actor–director Mel Ferrer (described by Beaton as 'a charming gangling man'), who has already been introduced to Hepburn by his friend Gregory Peck and describes her to Beaton as 'the biggest thing to come down the turnpike'. Hepburn has become aware of Ferrer through his recently released film *Lili*, which co-stars Leslie Caron, and which Hepburn enjoys so much that she goes to see it three times. Caron, two years younger than Hepburn, is also celebrated for her gamine hairstyle and boyish figure, and the pair represent a new look in comparison to the fuller-bodied appeal of American stars such as Marilyn Monroe and Jane Russell.

27 August: World premiere of *Roman Holiday* at Radio City Music Hall in New York.

GREGORY PECK and AUDREY HEPBURN in WILLIAM WYLER'S Production of
"ROMAN HOLIDAY"
with F. die Albert. Produced and Directed by William Wyler. Screenplay by Ian McLellan Hunter and John Dighton. Story by Ian McLellan Hunter. A Paramount Picture.

45

Fig. 45
With Gregory Peck in *Roman Holiday* (released 1953)

Fig. 46
With her Academy Award for Best Actress for *Roman Holiday*, 25 March 1954

Fig. 47
With her Tony Award for Best Actress for *Ondine*, photographed with Dolores Grey and Jo Van Fleet at the Plaza Hotel, New York, 30 March 1954

Fig. 48
Cover of *Time* magazine (7 September 1953 issue), illustrated by Boris Chaliapin

Fig. 49
Cover of Japanese monthly magazine *Eiga No Tomo* (May 1954)

Fig. 50
On horseback in costume as Joan of Arc with Mel Ferrer for the gala opening of the Ringling Brothers and Barnum & Bailey Circus in New York, 2 April 1954

2 September: *Roman Holiday* is released, on the same date as the British premiere.

7 September: An illustration of Hepburn by Boris Chaliapin showing her with an ice-cream cone appears as the cover of *Time* magazine. It is unprecedented in featuring a then relatively unknown subject on the cover.

September–November: As part of her Paramount contract, Hepburn makes a second film, *Sabrina*, the rights to which have been bought at her suggestion after seeing Samuel Taylor's play *Sabrina Fair* on Broadway. It is filmed over nine weeks at the Long Island estate of Paramount chairman Barney Balaban with further photography at Paramount Studios, Hollywood. Hepburn selects her own costumes from Hubert de Givenchy's Paris collection. Some of the most iconic images of Hepburn's career are taken in connection with *Sabrina*, including portrait studies by Bud Fraker for *Picturegoer* and Mark Shaw for *Life* magazine and pictures taken on set in Long Island and Wall Street by Dennis Stock.

1954
January: Hepburn has a two-week 'vacation' before moving to New York to begin rehearsals for *Ondine*, with director Alfred Lunt. The script, based on a 1939 play by Jean Giraudoux, is found by Ferrer and allows him to collaborate with Hepburn on stage.

18 February: *Ondine* opens on Broadway at the 46th Street Theatre and is a resounding hit.

24 March: After a performance of *Ondine*, Hepburn is driven across town to the NBC Century Theatre to attend the Academy Awards and receive the Oscar for Best Actress for her appearance in *Roman Holiday*; she also wins a BAFTA for her role.

28 March: Hepburn wins the Tony Award for Best Actress for her 'distinguished acting' in *Ondine* and is photographed at the Plaza Hotel with fellow winners Dolores Grey and Jo Van Fleet.

2 April: Hepburn makes an appearance riding a horse in her *Ondine* costume with Ferrer among guest performers at the first night of Ringling Bros and Barnum & Bailey Circus in New York. Opening night receipts go to the United States Palsy Fund.

May: Colour photographs on the front and back cover of Japanese monthly film magazine *Eiga No Tomo* reflect Hepburn's huge popularity in Japan, where her iconic haircut and style from *Roman Holiday* inspire thousands of fans even before any of her films are released there. Later in the year a gigantic float with a huge figure of Hepburn appears in the carnival parade for the winners of a beauty contest in her honour in the seaside resort of Kamakura.

46

47

TWENTY CENTS

SEPTEMBER 7, 1953

TIME
THE WEEKLY NEWSMAGAZINE

Boris Chaliapin

AUDREY HEPBURN
Behind the sparkle of rhinestones, a diamond's glow.

$6.00 A YEAR

(REG. U.S. PAT. OFF.)

VOL. LXII NO. 10

48

LEADING MOVIE MAGAZINE IN JAPAN ★ MAY 1954

映画の友

5

Audrey Hepburn
(Paramount)

EIGA NO TOMO

49

50

51

Fig. 51
Photographed in Rome on
the set of *War and Peace*
(released 1956)

Fig. 52
Nightclub scene from *Funny
Face*, with Fred Astaire

Fig. 53
Advertisement for NBC
television film *Mayerling*,
featuring Hepburn and Mel
Ferrer, broadcast on
4 February 1957

Roman Holiday earns back a third of its production costs in Japan alone, where it remains the favourite foreign film for many years, even out-grossing *Gone with the Wind*.

24 September: Hepburn marries Mel Ferrer in a civil ceremony, with a church wedding in Bürgenstock, on the shores of Lake Lucerne, Switzerland, the following day. Photographs taken by Magnum photographer Ernst Haas appear in British *Vogue*, *Picture Post* and other leading magazines.

November: A painting of Hepburn by Olga Lehmann illustrates the cover story in *Woman's Journal*. The text, by Britain's leading theatre critic Kenneth Tynan, states that she is 'the foremost Actress of the Year' and continues 'Audrey Hepburn is half fragility, half tenacity and all talent. We have scarcely heard the first of her.'

31 December: Hepburn and Ferrer fly into London where he is to appear in Michael Powell and Emeric Pressburger's film *Oh … Rosalinda!!* A Hepburn–Ferrer press reception and cocktail party is held at the Dorchester at 6pm that evening. While discussions with Powell and Pressburger to make a film version of *Ondine* continue, the film is widely announced in the press, notably in *Everybody's Weekly* magazine, which carries an exclusive colour photograph of Hepburn in costume at The Cloisters Museum, New York.

The British makers of *The Red Shoes* envision a retelling of the story, while Ferrer prefers a film of the theatre version. The project is eventually abandoned.

1955
April: Hepburn meets American film director King Vidor to discuss the making of *War and Peace*. Hepburn's agent Kurt Frings negotiates a fee of $350,000 plus weekly expenses of $500, then the highest salary for any female star. Hepburn and Ferrer change their permanent domicile to Switzerland.

1 July: Official start of filming of *War and Peace* at Cinecittà in Rome, with Hepburn starring as Natasha Rostova opposite Henry Fonda as Pierre Bezukhov and Ferrer as Prince Andrei. The film is produced by Dino de Laurentiis. Photographs on set are taken by Antony Beauchamp, Milton Greene and George Daniell and at Hepburn's temporary home, a rented farmhouse at Cecchina near Anzio, 20 miles from Rome, by Daniell, Philippe Halsman and Norman Parkinson.

18 July: Halsman's photographs, some of his most iconic portraits of Hepburn, appear in *Life* magazine.

December: Parkinson's photographs, showing Hepburn with the donkey Bimba, appear in *Glamour* magazine, accompanying Curtis Pepper's interview with Hepburn on the first anniversary of her marriage.

52

Audrey Hepburn and Mel Ferrer make their color TV debut in "Mayerling," produced, directed and staged by Anatole Litvak. See this absorbing, true story of Archduke Rudolph's star-crossed love affair—Monday, February 4, 8:00-9:30 pm, EST, on Producers' Showcase. 90 minutes, live, in color and black-and-white on NBC COLOR TELEVISION

53

1956

23 March: Yousuf Karsh (Karsh of Ottawa) takes portraits of Hepburn and Ferrer at Paramount Studios, where Hepburn is about to begin work on *Funny Face*. Karsh's portrait later inspires the Google Doodle celebrating the 85th anniversary of Hepburn's birth (2014), and a stamp featuring Hepburn is used by the Canadian postal service to celebrate Karsh's centenary (2008).

April: Hepburn begins filming *Funny Face*, in which she portrays a shy bookshop assistant who is discovered by a photographer and whisked off to Paris. The photographer, played by Fred Astaire, is based on Richard Avedon (who advised and worked on the film). Filming predominantly takes place in Hollywood, including the scenes at the Greenwich Village bookshop, with one month of filming exterior scenes in Paris.

August: After filming of *Funny Face* ends in July, Hepburn returns to Bürgenstock for a month's rest before travelling to Paris to begin her second film directed by Billy Wilder, *Love in the Afternoon*. As Ariane, the cellist daughter of a private detective played by Maurice Chevalier, she begins a romance with a playboy her father is investigating. Despite a classic final scene at a railway station, the public feel uncomfortable with the 28-year age gap between Hepburn and her love-interest, played by Gary Cooper. Stills and portrait photographs are taken by

Raymond Voinquel and George Konig; Sam Shaw and Walter Carone take additional on-set photographs.

1957

4 February: Premiere of lavish NBC TV production of *Mayerling*. Hepburn plays Maria Vestra, mistress of Crown Prince Rudolph, heir to the Habsburg Empire (Ferrer). She is drawn to the project by the prospect of working with her husband and with director Anatole Litvak, who has already made a successful version of the story. Her fee of $157,000 is a record for a television programme. It wins a large audience and a theatrical release in Europe, but Ferrer's performance is criticised. It is the couple's last appearance together on film.

December: Hepburn agrees to take the part of Sister Luke in Fred Zinnemann's film *The Nun's Story*. Based on the 1956 best-selling novel by Kathryn Hulme, the plot revolves around a Belgian nun who travels to the Congo in the 1930s to work at a mission hospital while struggling with her faith.

1958

January–March: Cast and crew begin filming in the Congo before returning to Rome for studio filming.

Keen to work with Ferrer as director on another project, Hepburn signs up for his adaptation of the W.H. Hudson book *Green Mansions: A Romance of the Tropical*

Forest. Hepburn plays a jungle girl called Rima who falls in love with an explorer. Stills are taken by Bob Willoughby, who also shoots a photo-essay of Hepburn at home in Hollywood with the fawn featured in the film. She names it 'Pippin', known for short as 'Ip'. Willoughby's photograph of Mel, Hepburn, 'Ip' and pet Yorkshire terrier on a sofa together becomes her Christmas card this year.

1959

28 January: In a bid to take on more challenging parts, Hepburn has accepted the role of Rachel, a Kiowa Indian by birth, in John Huston's Western *The Unforgiven*. Declining a stand-in, she is thrown from the stallion she is riding and breaks her back in four places; she is airlifted to Los Angeles and later has a miscarriage. The film is temporarily closed down until she recovers.

19 May: *Green Mansions* released. Despite being one of the first films shot in Panavision, it is generally deemed a critical failure.

18 July: *The Nun's Story* opens at Radio City Music Hall. It goes on to be one of Warner Bros most profitable films of the decade and receives eight Academy Award nominations, including Best Actress for Hepburn; she also wins awards from the New York Film Critics' Circle and BAFTA. *Films in Review* comments that 'her portrayal of Sister Luke is one of the great performances of the screen' and 'will

54

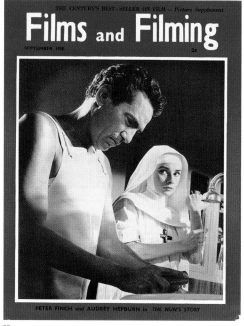

55

forever silence those who have thought her less an actress than a symbol of the sophisticated child-woman'.

September: Fashion shoot with Richard Avedon for *Harper's Bazaar* story 'Paris Pursuit: A Love Farce' also includes Buster Keaton, Art Buchwald and Mel Ferrer.

6 October: Hepburn begins a six-city tour to promote the European release of *The Nun's Story*. In Amsterdam she puts on a benefit for Dutch war veterans, whom she has long supported.

She visits Doorn, the location of the former Van Heemstra home, to supervise the unveiling of a lane named in her honour, 'Audrey Hepburnlaan'.

1960
6 April: *The Unforgiven* is released. Despite being compared to another adult Western, *Shane*, it is a critical and financial failure.

17 July: Hepburn gives birth to a son at Lucerne's municipal maternity hospital. He is named Sean, an Irish form of Ian, in honour of her brother.

28 July: The family appear almost immediately on a series of continental magazine covers, including that of the Italian weekly *Oggi*. Sean is christened in the church where his parents married and photographs are taken by Hepburn's friend Richard Avedon.

9 October: Filming for *Breakfast at Tiffany's* begins at 5am outside Tiffany's on Fifth Avenue, New York, as Hepburn emerges from a yellow taxi in a black evening dress. Director Blake Edwards has a deadline to complete the film's first scene before New York welcomes Russian President Nikita Khrushchev.

1961
5 October: *Breakfast at Tiffany's* released. Holly Golightly will become Hepburn's most famous role. George Axelrod's adaption of Truman Capote's short novella turns the leading character into a less obvious version of a call girl in what *New York Times* critic A.H. Weiler describes as 'a completely unbelievable but wholly captivating flight into fancy!' One of the most memorable scenes is Golightly singing Johnny Mercer and Henry Mancini's song 'Moon River', which goes on to win the Oscar for Best Song.

20 December: New York premiere of *The Children's Hour*, William Wyler's much-cherished project based on Lillian Hellman's play, which he had first filmed in 1936 as *These Three*. It is the most controversial role Hepburn has so far played and she agrees to take it partly out of loyalty to Wyler, who launched her career in *Roman Holiday*.

1962
Autumn: One day after finishing shooting *Paris When It Sizzles*, Hepburn begins filming *Charade* with Cary Grant as her

JOURS DE FRANCE

Audrey Hepburn l'actrice la plus élégante du monde

N° 376 - 1 NF
27 JANV. 1962

56

57

58

59

co-star. The Hitchcockian thriller is notable for its contemporary fashion designed for Hepburn by Givenchy.

1963
May: Hepburn and Ferrer are featured on the cover of French *Vogue* in a fashion shoot photographed by Bert Stern.

4 June: Press luncheon, held on Sound Stage Twelve at Warner Bros, to announce the start of work on *My Fair Lady*.

13 August: Filming begins. Still photographers on the set include Bob Willoughby and Mel Traxel. Hepburn is also photographed by Cecil Beaton, the film's costume designer, riding her bicycle (renamed Eliza), which had been given to her by Billy Wilder years before.

5 December: *Charade* released. It is nominated by prominent movie critic Pauline Kael as the best film of 1963, and Hepburn wins a BAFTA for Best Actress.

1964
April: Premiere of *Paris When It Sizzles*. It is the first film to credit a fragrance, L'Interdit, created by Givenchy for Hepburn. An image from the May 1963 *Vogue* photo shoot is used to launch the perfume.

21 October: World premiere of *My Fair Lady* at the Criterion Theatre on Broadway at 45th Street, New York.

22 December: Hepburn attends the Paris premiere for *My Fair Lady* at the Théâtre du Châtelet. Angela Williams and Pierluigi Praturlon photograph her in her suite at the Ritz, wearing a sky-blue brocade dress from Givenchy's autumn/winter collection.

1965
July: Hepburn returns to Paris to make a third film with William Wyler at the Boulogne Studios. In *How to Steal a Million* she stars alongside Peter O'Toole (shortly after his success in *Lawrence of Arabia*) in a comedy art-heist caper. Scenes in which O'Toole and Hepburn are locked in a cupboard take 11 days to film and become the subject of special on-set photographs by Terry O'Neill.

1966
Summer: Hepburn begins filming *Two for the Road* in the South of France, opposite Albert Finney. Directed by Stanley Donen and with a script by Frederic Raphael, the film breaks new ground for Hepburn's image and shows her in a wide selection of contemporary fashions by designers such as Paco Rabanne, Mary Quant and most prominently Ken Scott. Special publicity photographs are taken in St Tropez by Terry O'Neill and Pierluigi Praturlon.

1967
Early 1967: On Ferrer's recommendation Hepburn begins work on *Wait Until Dark*, based on a play by Frederick Knott, who had previously written *Dial M for Murder*. Ten days of filming take place on New York streets, while the rest of the film is made at Warner's Burbank studios. Directed by Terence Young, Hepburn plays a blind woman terrorised by three vicious criminals in her apartment in Greenwich Village.

1 September: The couple's lawyers announce that Hepburn and Ferrer are to divorce.

26 October: *Wait Until Dark* opens at Radio City Music Hall to record-breaking business, grossing $11 million and earning Hepburn a fifth Academy Award nomination for Best Actress (she had also been nominated for *Sabrina*, *The Nun's Story* and *Breakfast at Tiffany's*, as well as winning for *Roman Holiday*).

1968
June: Hepburn is invited on a cruise of the Greek Islands and on board meets Andrea Dotti, a young psychiatrist and assistant professor at the University of Rome.

5 December: Ferrer and Hepburn's final divorce decree is granted.

1969
18 January: Hepburn marries Dotti in Morges, Switzerland. They are photographed by Marcel Imsand, standing in the doorway of the city hall. Hepburn wears a pink jersey ensemble by Givenchy, with matching scarf. Her maid of honour and bride's witness are close friends Doris Brynner (wife of Yul) and actress Capucine.

62

63

1970

8 February: Hepburn's second son, Luca Dotti, is born at the cantonal hospital in Lausanne. For the next six years Hepburn devotes herself to being a full-time mother and supportive wife. She is concerned about the threat of kidnapping, which is prevalent in Italy, and torn between her desire to stay in peaceful Switzerland and Dotti's wish to remain in Rome, where he enjoys the nightlife.

1971

December: Invited by Marie-Hélène and Guy de Rothschild to a dance and dinner to mark the centenary of the birth of Marcel Proust, Hepburn wears a Valentino gown and is photographed by Cecil Beaton in a makeshift studio along with other guests, including Princess Grace of Monaco, Elizabeth Taylor and Capucine. Beaton's images are featured in American *Vogue* on 15 January 1972.

1975

Summer: Hepburn films *Robin and Marian*, directed by Richard Lester and co-starring Sean Connery, over 35 days in Spain. Scripted by James Goldman, it depicts an ageing Maid Marian and Robin Hood rekindling their love affair.

1976

11 March: *Robin and Marian* is released and provides a comeback for Hepburn, backed by a huge publicity campaign.

1979

Hepburn accepts the lead role in Terence Young's latest film, *Bloodline*, based on a novel by Sidney Sheldon, alongside an all-star cast including James Mason, Ben Gazzara, Omar Sharif and Romy Schneider. During filming in Sardinia and Copenhagen Hepburn forms a close relationship with her co-star Gazzara.

1980

June: Hepburn films *They All Laughed* on the streets of New York. The director, Peter Bogdanovich, wrote the script with her in mind and selects her character's costumes from Hepburn's own wardrobe. Ben Gazzara's involvement is an added incentive for her to take on the part. Sean Hepburn Ferrer appears in the cast opposite Dorothy Stratten, whose tragic murder in August overshadows the release of the film.

During filming Hepburn begins her relationship with Dutch-born actor Robert Wolders, widower of Hollywood star Merle Oberon. Wolders is to be Hepburn's partner for the rest of her life.

1981

January: Hepburn is photographed by Patrick Lichfield for his book *The Most Beautiful Women*.

Fig. 60
With Rex Harrison at the Los Angeles premiere of *My Fair Lady*

Fig. 61
Photographed by Angela Williams in her suite at the Ritz after the Paris premiere, of *My Fair Lady*, 28 October 1964

Fig. 62
With director Richard Lester on the set of *Robin and Marian* (released 1976)

Fig. 63
Hepburn and Sean Connery as Maid Marian and Robin Hood in *Robin and Marian*

64

65

66

Fig. 64
Hepburn with the cast of *They All Laughed* (released 1981); left to right: Colleen Camp, Blaine Novak, Patti Hansen, Ben Gazzara, Audrey Hepburn, John Ritter, Dorothy Stratten and George Morfogen

Fig. 65
With Robert Wagner in a publicity photograph by Douglas Kirkland for *Love Among Thieves* (released 1987)

Fig. 66
Publicity photo for *Bloodline* (released 1979)

Fig. 67
Cover of French *Elle* magazine (February 1993 issue) with Hepburn in her role as Goodwill Ambassador for UNICEF, photographed by Steven Meisel with, left to right: Karam Hider, Yoyo Zhang, Ralston O'Neill, Vijay Krishnan and Samson Mesghena

67

August: *They All Laughed* released. A failure at the time, the film has since become a cult hit and is listed by Quentin Tarantino among his favourite films.

1982
Hepburn is divorced from Andrea Dotti.

1987
February: Hepburn returns to acting in *Love Among Thieves*, a TV film for ABC, playing a concert pianist opposite Robert Wagner. She is again dressed by Givenchy. Publicity portraits are taken by Douglas Kirkland.

1988
9 March: Hepburn is appointed Special Ambassador for UNICEF, replacing Danny Kaye, who has died the previous year. Hepburn comments, 'I auditioned for this role for 45 years and I finally got it.' For the rest of her life she devotes herself to the work of UNICEF with eight highly effective international missions to help relieve third-world suffering. Among the countries she visits are Ethiopia (March 1988), Sudan (April 1989) and Bangladesh (October 1989). Her final field-trip is to Somalia in September 1992, which she describes as 'hell'.

1989
Hepburn accepts a cameo role in Steven Spielberg's film *Always*, a remake of the 1943 film *A Guy Named Joe* with a screenplay by Dalton Trumbo (the writer

of *Roman Holiday*). She acts opposite Richard Dreyfuss, playing the part of a guardian angel easing the passing of a crashed pilot.

1990
March: As part of her UNICEF work Hepburn collaborates with the composer Michael Tilson Thomas on a reading of selections from *The Diary of Anne Frank* with orchestral accompaniment. The performance tours five American cities.

April: Hepburn starts work on *Gardens of the World*, a ten-part PBS TV series which features gardens in seven countries including Japan and the Netherlands and is narrated by Michael York. (She was posthumously awarded an Emmy for the series.)

1991
22 April: Hepburn is honoured at the Film Society of Lincoln Center's 'Gala Tribute to Audrey Hepburn', where speeches are given by Billy Wilder, Gregory Peck and Anthony Perkins among others.

May: In one of her final major magazine features, Hepburn appears holding flowers as the cover star for *Vanity Fair*, as part of a portfolio of images by Steven Meisel. The profile and interview are by Dominick Dunne.

Hepburn travels to London to perform *Anne Frank* at the Barbican.

17 October: Hepburn and Hubert de Givenchy celebrate a forty-year professional association by posing for Jean-Claude Sauer for a story in *Paris Match*.

26 October: One of Sauer's images is also used on the cover of *Hello!* magazine.

1992
Early November: Hepburn is diagnosed with abdominal cancer. After undergoing unsuccessful surgery and treatment, she spends her last Christmas in Switzerland, surrounded by her family. She is awarded the US Presidential Medal of Freedom in December.

1993
20 January: Audrey Hepburn dies. The first episode of *Gardens of the World* airs the next day.

1 February: Worldwide coverage of Hepburn's life and career includes a cover story in French *Elle* using one of Meisel's 1991 photographs. She is shown surrounded by a group of children, illustrating her role as UNICEF Special Ambassador. It is the first of many magazines with a memorial feature paying tribute to her acting career and humanitarian achievements.

'Audrey has a tomboy's restless energy, but a natural grace and a lack of self-consciousness, which makes photographing her delightful.'

Antony Beauchamp

Further Reading

Books

- Cecil Beaton, *Cecil Beaton's Fair Lady* (Weidenfeld and Nicolson, London, 1964)
- Scott Brizel, *Audrey Hepburn: International Cover Girl (Her Life in Film and Fashion Through the Lens of Magazine Covers From Around the World)* (Titan Books Ltd, London, 2009)
- Howell Conant, *Audrey Hepburn in Breakfast at Tiffany's and Other Photographs* (Schirmer/Mosel, Munich, 2007)
- Luca Dotti, *Audrey In Rome* (edited by Ludovica Damiani, with text by Sciascia Gambaccini) (Harper Design, London, 2012)
- Ellen Erwin and Jessica Z. Diamond, *The Audrey Hepburn Treasures* (Atria Books, New York, 2006)
- Sean Hepburn Ferrer, *Audrey Hepburn: An Elegant Spirit* (Sidgwick and Jackson, London, 2003)
- Ellen Fontana (with a foreword by Sean Hepburn Ferrer), *Audrey 100: A Rare and Intimate Photo Collection Selected by Audrey Hepburn's Family* (New Holland, London, 2010)
- Sarah Gristwood, *Breakfast at Tiffany's: The Official 50th Anniversary Companion* (Skira Rizzoli, New York, 2011)
- Charles Higham, *Audrey: The Life of Audrey Hepburn* (Macmillan Publishing, New York, 1984)
- Robyn Karney, *A Star Danced: The Life of Audrey Hepburn* (Bloomsbury Publishing Ltd, London, 1993)
- Pamela Clarke Keogh, *Audrey Style* (HarperCollins, London, 1999)

- Caroline Latham, *Audrey Hepburn* (Proteus, New York, 1984)
- June Marsh, *Audrey Hepburn in Hats* (Reel Art Press, London, 2013) Sheridan Morley, *Audrey Hepburn:*
- *A Celebration* (Pavilion Books, London, 1993)
- Rachel Moseley, *Growing Up With Audrey Hepburn* (Manchester University Press, 2002)
- Tony Nourmand, *Audrey Hepburn: The Paramount Years* (with a foreword by Professor Sir Christopher Frayling) (Boxtree, London, 2006)
- Barry Paris, *Audrey Hepburn* (Weidenfeld & Nicolson, London, 1997)
- Klaus-Jurgen Sembach, *Adieu Audrey: Memories of Audrey Hepburn* (Schirmer Art Books/Schirmer/Mosel, Munich, 1993)
- Mark Shaw, *Charmed by Audrey: Life on the Set of Sabrina* (Insight Editions, New York, 2008)
- Donald Spoto, *Enchantment: The Life of Audrey Hepburn* (Hutchinson, London, 2006)
- Jerry Vermilye, *The Complete Films of Audrey Hepburn: Her Life and Career* (Citadel Press, New York, 1996)
- Alexander Walker, *Audrey: The Real Story* (revised and expanded edition, Orion Books, London, 1995)
- Sam Wasson, *5th Avenue, 5am: Breakfast at Tiffany's and the Dawn of the Modern Woman* (HarperCollins, London, 2010)
- Bob Willoughby, *Audrey: An Intimate Collection* (Vision On, London, 2002)

- Bob Willoughby, *Audrey Hepburn Photographs 1953–1966* (Taschen, Cologne, 2014)
- Bob Willoughby, *Remembering Audrey* (Life Great Photographers Series, Life Books, New York, 2008)
- David Wills and Stephen Schmidt, *Audrey: The 60s* (HarperCollins, London, 2012)
- Ian Woodward, *Audrey Hepburn* (W.H. Allen, London, 1984)
- Nick Yapp, *Audrey Hepburn* (Endeavor London Ltd, 2009)

Selected magazine articles

- 'We Take a Girl to Look for Spring', *Picture Post* (13 May 1950)
- John Bretton, 'She's a Young Wives' Tale' in *Picturegoer* (16 December 1950)
- Charles Hamblett, 'Audrey – the other Hepburn', *Illustrated* (2 June 1951)
- Colette, 'Hepburn … and Hepburn', *American Weekly* (23 March 1952)
- Jack Hamilton, 'Audrey – the new Hepburn' in *Look* (21 October 1952)
- Paul Ridgway, 'Watch Out Audrey – Full Steam Ahead' in *Picturegoer* (20 June 1953)
- Dennis Myers, 'Audrey Steps into the Starlight' in *Picturegoer* (29 August 1953)
- David Clayton, '"Princess" Audrey' in *Illustrated* (5 September 1953)
- 'Princess Apparent', cover story in *Time* (7 September 1953)
- 'Audrey Hepburn, Many-Sided Charmer: Photographs by Mark Shaw' in *Life* (7 Dec 1953)
- Bill Tusher, 'Candy Pants Princess: The Dramatic Life Story of Thrilling Little Audrey Hepburn – Hollywood's Most Sensational Personality' in *Motion Picture* (February 1954)
- 'What They Are Saying about Audrey Hepburn', in *Illustrated* (11 September 1954), with quotations by Cecil Landeau, Angus McBean and Marie Rambert Cecil Beaton, 'Audrey Hepburn' in British *Vogue* (October 1954)
- Kenneth Tynan, 'Audrey Hepburn: Foremost Actress of the Year' in *Woman's Journal* (November 1954)

- Antony Beauchamp, 'Audrey Hepburn's Charm', *Illustrated* (29 January 1955)
- 'Audrey Hepburn Interviews Herself', *Good Taste* (April 1955)
- George Borden, 'The "Phony" Discovery of Audrey Hepburn' in *Secret Life* (April 1956)
- Robert Muller, 'Audrey Dances with Astaire' in *Picture Post* (7 July 1956)
- '*War and Peace* Starring Audrey Hepburn and Henry Fonda' in *Screen Stories* (October 1956)
- David Stone, 'A Star's Private Life', *Everybody's* (20 October 1956)
- S.L. Solon, 'Little Girl Found' in *Men Only* (July 1957)
- Mel Ferrer, 'Audrey…' in *Modern Woman* (December 1959)
- Donald Zec, 'Audrey Hepburn's Own Story' in *Woman's Illustrated* (1 October 1960)
- 'An Orchid that Grew in a Farmyard' in *Life* (international edition, 9 October 1961)
- 'She … is One of the Original Innocents', *Woman's Journal* (11 April 1962)
- Rowland Barber, 'The Delightful Riddle of Audrey Hepburn' in *Good Housekeeping* (August 1962)
- 'Audrey Hepburn: What Comes Next?', *Woman's Journal* (January 1966)
- 'Look At Audrey Now!', *Ladies' Home Journal* (January 1967)
- Joseph Barry, 'Audrey Hepburn at 40' in *McCall's* (July 1969)
- 'Audrey Hepburn: Star in a Givenchy Heaven'. British *Vogue* (1 March 1971)

- Curtis Bill Pepper, 'The Loving World of Audrey Hepburn Dotti', British *Vogue* (June 1971)
- Gene Ringgold, 'Audrey Hepburn Added Post-War Realism to the Movies' Image of the Child-Woman' in *Films in Review* (December 1971)
- Jim Watters, 'The Voice, The Neck, The Charm: They Just Don't Make Movie Stars Like Audrey Hepburn Anymore' in *People Weekly* (12 April 1976)
- Marilyn Willison, 'The Divine Miss Hepburn' in *Marie Claire* (September 1988)
- 'That Girl with the Eyes' in *Interview* (August 1990) – quotations by nine Audrey Hepburn fans including Richard Avedon, Hubert de Givenchy and Marc Jacobs Dominick Dunne, 'Hepburn Heart' in *Vanity Fair* (May 1991)
- Curtis Bill Pepper, 'A Tribute to Audrey Hepburn' in *People Extra* (Winter 1993)

Picture Credits

Frontispiece: Photographed by Philippe Halsman near Rome for *Life* (cover portrait, 18 July 1955 issue) (detail of cat. 35)

p.5: Hepburn (far right) in *Christmas Party*, a revue at the Cambridge Theatre, London, 9 December 1949 (detail of fig. 36)

p.7: Photographed by Larry Fried in an automat in New York during rehearsals for *Gigi*, late 1951 (detail of fig. 43)

p.11: Nightclub scene from *Funny Face*, with Fred Astaire (detail of fig. 52)

p.18: Photographed by Cecil Beaton, 29 March 1954 (detail of cat. 56)

p.191: Hepburn dancing at Ciro's, London, 1950.© reserved. Audrey Hepburn Estate/ Luca Dotti & Sean Hepburn Ferrer.

Fig. 1: Paramount/The Kobal Collection.
Fig. 2: © DACS 2015.
Fig. 3: © reserved. TP Research Collection. Image courtesy National Portrait Gallery, London.
Fig. 4: © Hulton Archive/Bert Hardy/ *Picture Post*/Getty Images. TP Research Collection. Image courtesy National Portrait Gallery, London.
Fig. 5: © Bert Hardy/*Picture Post*/Getty Images. TP Research Collection. Image courtesy National Portrait Gallery, London.
Fig. 6: © reserved. Audrey Hepburn Estate/Luca Dotti & Sean Hepburn Ferrer.
Fig. 7: TP Research Collection. Image courtesy Paramount/National Portrait Gallery, London.
Fig. 8: © Mirrorpix. TP Research Collection. Image courtesy National Portrait Gallery, London.
Fig. 9: © David Seymour/Magnum Photos.
Fig. 10: © Mark Shaw/mptvimages.com.
Fig. 11: © reserved. TP Research Collection. Image courtesy National Portrait Gallery, London.
Fig. 12: © reserved. Audrey Hepburn Estate/Luca Dotti & Sean Hepburn Ferrer.
Fig. 13: *Funny Face*/Paramount. Image courtesy Philippe Garner.
Fig. 14: © reserved. Audrey Hepburn Estate/Luca Dotti & Sean Hepburn Ferrer.
Fig. 15: Photographs by Richard Avedon. Copyright © The Richard Avedon Foundation.
Fig. 16: *Two for the Road*/20th Century Fox. TP Research Collection. Image courtesy National Portrait Gallery, London.
Fig. 17: © Henry Wolf. Image courtesy The Richard Avedon Foundation.
Fig. 18: *Breakfast at Tiffany's*/Paramount. TP Research Collection. Image courtesy National Portrait Gallery, London.
Fig. 19: © reserved. TP Research Collection. Image courtesy National Portrait Gallery, London.
Fig. 20: © George Douglas/TopFoto. TP Research Collection. Image courtesy National Portrait Gallery, London.
Fig. 21: © reserved. TP Research Collection. Image courtesy Repropress/ National Portrait Gallery, London.
Fig. 22: © reserved. TP Research Collection. Image courtesy Time Life/ National Portrait Gallery, London.
Fig. 23: © reserved. TP Research Collection. Image courtesy Playbill/National Portrait Gallery, London.
Fig. 24: *Funny Face*/Paramount. TP Research Collection. Image courtesy National Portrait Gallery, London.
Fig. 25: *The Unforgiven*/Hill-Hecht-Lancaster Productions. TP Research Collection. Image courtesy National Portrait Gallery, London.
Fig. 26: TP Research Collection. Image courtesy Time Life/National Portrait Gallery, London.
Fig. 27: *Charade*/Universal/The Kobal Collection.
Fig. 28: © Bert Stern/*Vogue* Paris. TP Research Collection.
Fig. 29: © reserved. Photograph by Jerome Ltd. Audrey Hepburn Estate/Luca Dotti & Sean Hepburn Ferrer.
Fig. 30: © reserved. Audrey Hepburn Estate/Luca Dotti & Sean Hepburn Ferrer.
Fig. 31: © reserved. Audrey Hepburn Estate/Luca Dotti & Sean Hepburn Ferrer.
Fig. 32: © reserved. TP Research Collection. Image courtesy National Portrait Gallery, London.
Fig. 33: © reserved. TP Research Collection. Image courtesy National Portrait Gallery, London.
Fig. 34: © reserved. TP Research Collection. Image courtesy National Portrait Gallery, London.

Fig. 35: © Illustrated London News Ltd/ Mary Evans.
Fig. 36 (and p.5): Matthew Cunningham Collection. Image courtesy National Portrait Gallery, London.
Fig. 37: *The Lavender Hill Mob*/Ealing Studios. TP Research Collection. Image courtesy National Portrait Gallery, London.
Fig. 38: © reserved. TP Research Collection. Image courtesy National Portrait Gallery, London.
Fig. 39: © Mirrorpix. TP Research Collection.
Fig. 40: © reserved. TP Research Collection. Image courtesy National Portrait Gallery, London.
Fig. 41: © Bettman/Corbis.
Fig. 42: © Lawrence Fried Photography. All rights reserved.
Fig. 43 (and p.7): © Lawrence Fried Photography. All rights reserved.
Fig. 44: © reserved. TP Research Collection. Image courtesy National Portrait Gallery, London.
Fig. 45: *Roman Holiday*/Paramount. TP Research Collection. Image courtesy National Portrait Gallery, London.
Fig. 46: Press Association Images.
Fig. 47: © Bettmann/Corbis.
Fig. 48: © reserved. TP Research Collection. Image courtesy Time Life/ National Portrait Gallery, London.
Fig. 49: © reserved. TP Research Collection. Image courtesy National Portrait Gallery, London.
Fig. 50: © Bettman/Corbis.
Fig. 51: *War and Peace*/Paramount. TP Research Collection. Image courtesy National Portrait Gallery, London.

Fig. 52 (and p.11): *Funny Face*/Paramount. TP Research Collection. Image courtesy National Portrait Gallery, London.
Fig. 53. © reserved. TP Research Collection. Image courtesy National Portrait Gallery, London.
Fig. 54. © Bettmann/Corbis. TP Research Collection.
Fig. 55. © reserved. *The Nun's Story*/ Warner Bros. TP Research Collection. Image courtesy National Portrait Gallery, London.
Fig. 56: Madame Figaro/Camera Press with the authorisation of Le Figaro. TP Research Collection.
Fig. 57: *Breakfast at Tiffany's*/Jurow-Shepherd. TP Research Collection.
Fig. 58: *Paris When It Sizzles*/Richard Quine Productions/George Axelrod Productions. TP Research Collection. Image courtesy National Portrait Gallery, London.
Fig. 59: *Charade*/Universal. TP Research Collection. Image courtesy National Portrait Gallery, London.
Fig. 60: © reserved. TP Research Collection. Image courtesy National Portrait Gallery, London.
Fig. 61 (and p.154): © Angela Williams/ AWA. TP Research Collection.
Fig. 62: *Robin and Marian*/Columbia. TP Research Collection. Image courtesy National Portrait Gallery, London.
Fig. 63: *Robin and Marian*/Columbia. TP Research Collection. Image courtesy National Portrait Gallery, London.
Fig. 64: *They All Laughed*/Moon Pictures/ Time Life Films. TP Research Collection.

Image courtesy National Portrait Gallery, London.
Fig. 65: *Love Among Thieves*/Lorimar Productions/Robert Papazian Productions. TP Research Collection. Image courtesy National Portrait Gallery, London.
Fig. 66: *Bloodline*/Paramount. TP Research Collection. Image courtesy National Portrait Gallery, London.
Fig. 67: © Steven Meisel/Art + Commerce. Steven Meisel for ELLE FRANCE. TP Research Collection. Image courtesy National Portrait Gallery, London.

Exhibition Works

1. Audrey Hepburn, 1938. Audrey Hepburn Estate/Luca Dotti & Sean Hepburn Ferrer. Image © reserved.
2. Dance recital photograph by Manon van Suchtelen, 14 April 1942. Audrey Hepburn Estate/Luca Dotti & Sean Hepburn Ferrer. Image © reserved.
3. Ballet school recital in Arnhem, Netherlands, 1944. Audrey Hepburn Estate/Luca Dotti & Sean Hepburn Ferrer. Image © reserved.
4. Audrey Hepburn (far left) at a ballet class durung the Second World War, photographed by Arnold Bouvet, 1944. Audrey Hepburn Estate/Luca Dotti & Sean Hepburn Ferrer. Image © reserved.
5. Audrey Hepburn shortly after the liberation of the Netherlands, 1946. Audrey Hepburn Estate/Luca Dotti & Sean Hepburn Ferrer. Image © reserved.
6. Fashion photograph by Antony Beauchamp, 1949. Audrey Hepburn

Estate/Luca Dotti & Sean Hepburn Ferrer. Image © reserved.

7. Fashion photograph by Antony Beauchamp, 1949. Matthew Cunningham Collection. © reserved. Image courtesy National Portrait Gallery, London. Photography: Victoria Miller.

8 (and p.46). Photographed by Bert Hardy in Kew Gardens, London, on 30 April 1950 for *Picture Post* (13 May 1950 issue). The Hulton Archive. Image © Bert Hardy/Getty Images.

9. Unpublished photograph by Bert Hardy taken in Richmond Park, London, on 30 April 1950 for *Picture Post*. The Hulton Archive. Image © Bert Hardy/Getty Images.

10. Cast photograph for *Sauce Tartare* at the Cambridge Theatre, London, by Angus McBean, June 1949. Audrey Hepburn Estate/Luca Dotti & Sean Hepburn Ferrer. Image © Harvard Theatre Collection, Houghton Library, Harvard University.

11. Programme cover for Cecil Landeau's *Petite Sauce Tartare* at Ciro's Club, London, photograph by Angus McBean, 1949. Bob Cooper. Image © Harvard Theatre Collection, Houghton Library, Harvard University.

12. Advertising photograph for Lacto-Calamine by Angus McBean, November 1950. National Portrait Gallery, London (NPG x132853). Courtesy of Adrian Woodhouse. Image © Adrian Woodhouse.

13. Advertising photograph for Lacto-Calamine by Angus McBean, October 1950. National Portrait Gallery, London (NPG P1295). Image © reserved.

14. Audrey Hepburn in *Secret People*,
cover of *The Dancing Times* (March 1952 issue). Bob Cooper. Image courtesy Studiocanal Films Ltd/National Portrait Gallery, London. Photography: Victoria Miller.

15. Audrey Hepburn and Colette, press photograph for *France-Soir*, Paris, 1951. Audrey Hepburn Estate/Luca Dotti & Sean Hepburn Ferrer. Image © reserved.

16. Audrey Hepburn photographed in costume as Gigi at the Fulton Theatre, New York, by Norman Parkinson, January 1952. Norman Parkinson Ltd/Courtesy Norman Parkinson Archive. Image © Norman Parkinson Ltd/Courtesy Norman Parkinson Archive.

17. Audrey Hepburn photographed in her dressing room for *Gigi* at the Fulton Theatre, New York, by Larry Fried, 1951. TP Research Collection. Image © 2015 Lawrence Fried Photography. Image courtesy National Portrait Gallery, London. Photography: Emma Cavalier.

18. Unpublished photograph of Audrey Hepburn at Rockefeller Center, New York, by George Douglas, March 1952. The George Douglas Archive. Image © George Douglas/Topfoto.

19. Photographed by Irving Penn in Paris for American *Vogue* (1 November 1951 issue). Audrey Hepburn Estate/Luca Dotti & Sean Hepburn Ferrer. Image © Condé Nast.

20. Photographed wearing a hat made by Mr Fred, designed and photographed by Erwin Blumenfeld, 1952. Private Collection. Image © The Estate of Erwin Blumenfeld.

21. William Wyler directing Audrey
Hepburn and Gregory Peck on the Spanish Steps for *Roman Holiday* (released 1953). Matthew Cunningham Collection. Image courtesy National Portrait Gallery, London. Photography: Victoria Miller.

22 and 23. Costume tests for *Sabrina* (Paramount Pictures, released 1954), 21 September 1953. Audrey Hepburn Estate/ Luca Dotti & Sean Hepburn Ferrer. Image © reserved.

24. Publicity portrait by Bud Fraker for *Sabrina* (released 1954). TP Research Collection. Image © Bettman/Corbis; courtesy National Portrait Gallery, London.

25. Bud Fraker photographing Audrey Hepburn in the Paramount Studio portrait gallery, Hollywood, photographed by Bob Willoughby, 1953. Bob Willoughby Photography. Image © Bob Willoughby Photography.

26. Publicity portrait by Bud Fraker for *Sabrina* (released 1954). Matthew Cunningham Collection. Image © Underwood & Underwood/Corbis. Image courtesy National Portrait Gallery, London. Photography: Victoria Miller.

27. Photographed by Mark Shaw outside Hepburn's Beverly Hills apartment during the filming of *Sabrina*, for a photo-essay in *Life* (7 December 1953 issue). The Mark Shaw Photographic Archive. Image © Mark Shaw/mptvimages.com.

28 (and p.62). Photographed in New York by Dennis Stock during the filming of *Sabrina* (released 1954). Peter Fetterman Gallery Collection. Image © Magnum Photos London/New York.

29. Photographed by Philippe Halsman as

Ondine, 1954. Audrey Hepburn Estate/Luca Dotti & Sean Hepburn Ferrer. © Philippe Halsman/Magnum Photos.

30. Audrey Hepburn photographed by Richard Avedon, New York, 18 December 1953. Audrey Hepburn Estate/Luca Dotti & Sean Hepburn Ferrer. Copyright © The Richard Avedon Foundation.

31. Audrey Hepburn photographed by Mark Shaw preparing for Ondine in her dressing room at the Forty-Sixth Street Theatre, New York, published in Mademoiselle (June 1954 issue). The Mark Shaw Photographic Archive. Image © Mark Shaw/mptvimages.com.

32 (and p.174). Photographed by Antony Beauchamp, 1955. Audrey Hepburn Estate/Luca Dotti & Sean Hepburn Ferrer. Image © reserved.

33. Photographed by Antony Beauchamp, 1955. Audrey Hepburn Estate/Luca Dotti & Sean Hepburn Ferrer. Image © reserved.

34. Photographed by Philippe Halsman near Rome for Life (18 July 1955 issue). Audrey Hepburn Estate/Luca Dotti & Sean Hepburn Ferrer. Image © Philippe Halsman/Magnum Photos.

35 (and frontispiece). Photographed by Philippe Halsman near Rome for Life (cover portrait, 18 July 1955 issue). Audrey Hepburn Estate/Luca Dotti & Sean Hepburn Ferrer. Image © Philippe Halsman/Magnum Photos.

36. Photographed by Norman Parkinson with Bimba the donkey at the Villa Rolli, Cecchina, near Rome, during the filming of War and Peace (released 1956), 23 June 1955. National Portrait Gallery, London (NPG x30114). Image © Norman Parkinson Ltd/Courtesy Norman Parkinson Archive.

37 (and front cover). Photographed by Jack Cardiff during the filming of War and Peace (released 1956). Simon Regan Collection (www.reganprint.com). Image © Jack Cardiff.

38 (and back cover). Photographed by Norman Parkinson wearing Givenchy at the Villa Rolli, Cecchina, near Rome, during the filming of War and Peace (released 1956), June 1955. Norman Parkinson Ltd/Courtesy Norman Parkinson Archive. Image © Norman Parkinson Ltd/Courtesy Norman Parkinson Archive.

39. Street scene in Italy photographed by George Daniell, 1955, showing Audrey Hepburn in posters for Lux soap (advertising photographs by Bud Fraker). Audrey Hepburn Estate/Luca Dotti & Sean Hepburn Ferrer. Image © George Daniell Archive and Dwayne and Gina DeJoy.

40. Photographed by George Daniell on the set of War and Peace (released 1956). Audrey Hepburn Estate/Luca Dotti & Sean Hepburn Ferrer. Image © George Daniell Archive and Dwayne and Gina DeJoy.

41. Publicity portrait by Bud Fraker for Funny Face (released 1957). Audrey Hepburn Estate/Luca Dotti & Sean Hepburn Ferrer.

42. Photographed by Yousuf Karsh, Paramount Studios, Hollywood, 26 March 1956. Museum of Fine Arts, Boston. Gift of Estrellita and Yousuf Karsh. Courtesy of Camera Press. Image © Estate of Yousuf Karsh.

43. Photographed by Sam Shaw during the filming of Love in the Afternoon, 1956. The Sam Shaw Family Archives. Image © Sam Shaw Inc./www.shawfamilyarchives.com.

44. Photographed by Sam Shaw during the filming of Love in the Afternoon, 1956. Audrey Hepburn Estate/Luca Dotti & Sean Hepburn Ferrer. Image © Sam Shaw Inc./www.shawfamilyarchives.com.

45. Photographed by George Konig on location in the grounds of the Château Vitry, near Paris, for Love in the Afternoon (released 1957). Audrey Hepburn Estate/Luca Dotti & Sean Hepburn Ferrer. Image © reserved.

46. Photographed by Raymond Voinquel for Love in the Afternoon (released 1957). Audrey Hepburn Estate/Luca Dotti & Sean Hepburn Ferrer. Image © reserved.

47. Photographed by Leo Fuchs on location in Africa for The Nun's Story, 1958. Audrey Hepburn Estate/Luca Dotti & Sean Hepburn Ferrer. Image © Leo Fuchs Photography Archives.

48. Photographed by Hamilton Millard on location in Africa for The Nun's Story, 1958. TP Research Collection. Image © Estate of Hamilton Millard. Image courtesy National Portrait Gallery, London. Photography: Emma Cavalier.

49. Mel Ferrer directing Audrey Hepburn on the set of Green Mansions at MGM studios, Hollywood, photographed by Bob Willoughby, 1958. Audrey Hepburn Estate/Luca Dotti & Sean Hepburn Ferrer. Image © Bob Willoughby Photography.

50. Audrey Hepburn with her fawn, Ip, in Gelson's supermarket, Beverly Hills,

at the time of filming *Green Mansions*, photographed by Bob Willoughby, 1958. Audrey Hepburn Estate/Luca Dotti & Sean Hepburn Ferrer. Image © Bob Willoughby Photography.

51. Photographed by Phil Stern on location in Mexico filming *The Unforgiven* (released 1960). TP Research Collection. Image © reserved. Image courtesy National Portrait Gallery, London. Photography: Emma Cavalier.

52. Drawing of Audrey Hepburn by Cecil Beaton, 1954. Private Collection of Sean H. Ferrer. Image © National Portrait Gallery, London.

53. Audrey Hepburn and Richard Avedon, 1956. Audrey Hepburn Estate/Luca Dotti & Sean Hepburn Ferrer. Courtesy The Richard Avedon Foundation. © Gerard Decaux.

54. Photograph by Richard Avedon showing Audrey Hepburn with a drawing of her by Rufino Tamayo (made in 1957). Audrey Hepburn Estate/Luca Dotti & Sean Hepburn Ferrer. Copyright © The Richard Avedon Foundation. Drawing of Audrey Hepburn by Rufino Tamayo; © Estate of the artist in support of Fundación Olga Y Rufino Tamayo, A.C.

55. Audrey Hepburn and Art Buchwald with Simone d'Aillencourt, Frederick Eberstadt, Barbara Mullen and Dr Reginald Kernan. Evening dresses by Balmain, Dior and Patou. Photograph by Richard Avedon, Maxim's, Paris, August 1959. Audrey Hepburn Estate/Luca Dotti & Sean Hepburn Ferrer. Copyright © The Richard Avedon Foundation.

56 (and p.18): Photographed by Cecil Beaton, 29 March 1954. The Cecil Beaton Studio Archive at Sotheby's. Image © The Cecil Beaton Studio Archive at Sotheby's.

57. Photographed by Cecil Beaton at the Hassler Hotel, Rome, January 1960. The Cecil Beaton Studio Archive at Sotheby's. Image © The Cecil Beaton Studio Archive at Sotheby's.

58. Audrey Hepburn as Holly Golightly at Tiffany's Fifth Avenue, New York, during the filming of *Breakfast at Tiffany's* (released 1961), photographed by Howell Conant. The Howell Conant Archive. Image © Howell Conant/Bob Adelman Books, Inc.

59. Audrey Hepburn as Holly Golightly, photographed by Howell Conant in his New York studio, 1960. The Howell Conant Archive. Image © Howell Conant/Bob Adelman Books, Inc.

60. Audrey Hepburn as Holly Golightly on set during the filming of *Breakfast at Tiffany's* (released 1961), photographed by Howell Conant. Howell Conant Archive. Image © Howell Conant/Bob Adelman Books, Inc.

61. Audrey Hepburn and Mel Ferrer photographed by Pierluigi Praturlon, 1961. Audrey Hepburn Estate/Luca Dotti & Sean Hepburn Ferrer. Image © reserved.

62. Photographed by Vincent Rossell, wearing a Givenchy ski suit for *Charade* (released 1963). TP Research Collection. Image courtesy National Portrait Gallery, London. Photography: Emma Cavalier. Image © Vincent Rossell.

63. Audrey Hepburn wearing an ensemble designed by Cecil Beaton for *My Fair Lady* (released 1964), photographed by Beaton, 1963. The Cecil Beaton Studio Archive at Sotheby's. Image © The Cecil Beaton Studio Archive at Sotheby's.

64. Audrey Hepburn on the set of *My Fair Lady* (released 1964) with her dog, Assam, photographed by Cecil Beaton, 1963. The Cecil Beaton Studio Archive at Sotheby's. Image © The Cecil Beaton Studio Archive at Sotheby's.

65. Audrey Hepburn dressed in Givenchy with sunglasses by Oliver Goldsmith, photographed by Douglas Kirkland for *How to Steal a Million* (released 1966). Iconic Images/Douglas Kirkland. Image © Douglas Kirkland.

66. Audrey Hepburn with Peter O'Toole, photographed by Terry O'Neill during the filming of *How to Steal a Million* (released 1966). Iconic Images/Terry O'Neill. Image © Iconic Images.

67 (and p.122). Audrey Hepburn wearing an ensemble by Michèle Rosier for V de V and boots by Céline, photographed by William Klein for American *Vogue* (January 1966 isssue). Image © William Klein.

68. Publicity portrait with Albert Finney for *Two for the Road* (released 1967). TP Research Collection. *Two for the Road*/Stanley Donen Films.

69. Photographed by Terry O'Neill on location for *Two for the Road* (released 1967). Iconic Images/Terry O'Neill. Image © Iconic Images.

70. Publicity portrait with Shirley MacLaine and James Garner for *The Children's Hour* (released 1961). TP Research Collection. Image courtesy National Portrait Gallery, London.

71. Photographed by Howell Conant at the time of *Wait Until Dark* (released 1967). Howell Conant Archive. Image © Howell Conant/Bob Adelman Books, Inc.

72. Photographed wearing Givenchy by Henry Clarke for British *Vogue* (1 March 1971). Henry Clarke/*Vogue*. Image © The Condé Nast Publications Ltd.

73. Photographed at home in Rome by Elisabetta Catalano, 1975. Audrey Hepburn Estate/Luca Dotti & Sean Hepburn Ferrer. Image © Elisabetta Catalano.

74. Photographed with Hubert de Givenchy at the Hotel Lancaster, Paris, by Victor Skrebneski, 18 November 1986. Image © Skrebneski Photograph.

75. Photographed on location in Paris with Ben Gazzara for Sidney Sheldon's *Bloodline* (released 1979). TP Research Collection. Image courtesy National Portrait Gallery, London.

76. Publicity photograph by John Shannon for Steven Spielberg's *Always* (released 1989). TP Research Collection. Image courtesy National Portrait Gallery, London.

77 (and p.142). Photographed by Steven Meisel for *Vanity Fair* (May 1991 issue). Audrey Hepburn Estate/Luca Dotti & Sean Hepburn Ferrer. Image © Steven Meisel/Art + Commerce.

78. Photographed by Steven Meisel for *Vanity Fair* (May 1991 issue). Audrey Hepburn Estate/Luca Dotti & Sean Hepburn Ferrer. Image © Steven Meisel/Art + Commerce.

79. Photographed by Robert Wolders during a UNICEF mission to Sudan, 1989. Hepburn Estate/Luca Dotti & Sean Hepburn Ferrer. Image © Robert Wolders.

80. Photographed by Betty Press during a UNICEF mission to Somalia, 1992. Hepburn Estate/Luca Dotti & Sean Hepburn Ferrer. Image © Betty Press/UNICEF.

Index

List of Lenders

The Cecil Beaton Studio Archive at Sotheby's
The Howell Conant Archive
Condé Nast Archive, London
Robert Cooper
Matthew Cunningham Collection
The George Douglas Archive
Private Collection of Sean H. Ferrer
Peter Fetterman Gallery Collection
Philippe Garner
Audrey Hepburn Estate
The Hulton Archive
Iconic Images
William Klein Studio
Museum of Fine Arts, Boston
The Norman Parkinson Archive
Private Collection
Simon Regan Collection
The Mark Shaw Photographic Archive
The Sam Shaw Family Archives
Skrebneski, Inc.
TP Research Collection
Christopher Willoughby

Published in Great Britain by
National Portrait Gallery Publications,
St Martin's Place, London WC2H 0HE

Published to accompany the exhibition
Audrey Hepburn: Portraits of an Icon
at the National Portrait Gallery, London,
from 2 July to 18 October 2015, and
The Wilson, Cheltenham Art Gallery &
Museum, from November 2015 to
January 2016.

This exhibition has been made possible
by the provision of insurance through
the Government Indemnity Scheme.
The National Portrait Gallery, London,
would like to thank HM Government for
providing Government Indemnity and the
Department of Culture, Media and Sport
and Arts Council England for arranging
the indemnity.

Your purchase supports the National
Portrait Gallery, London. For a complete
catalogue of current publications, please
write to the National Portrait Gallery at the
address above, or visit our website at www.
npg.org.uk/publications

ISBN 978 1 85514 497 2 hardback
ISBN 978 1 85514 575 7 paperback

A catalogue record for this book is
available from the British Library.

10 9 8 7 6 5 4 3 2 1

Printed and bound in Italy

Managing Editor: Christopher Tinker
Senior Editor: Sarah Ruddick
Picture research: Kathleen Bloomfield
Production Manager: Ruth Müller-Wirth
Design: Osborne Ross

Organised with support from
the Audrey Hepburn Estate/
Luca Dotti & Sean Hepburn Ferrer

With the generous support of
the *Audrey Hepburn* Exhibition
Supporters Group

FSC
www.fsc.org
MIX
Paper from
responsible sources
FSC® C015829